WITHDRAWN

THRESHOLD

The First Days of Retirement

Recording some of the disappointments,
pleasures, and reflections of a new
traveler into that state of joblessness
sometimes known as the Golden Age

Alan H. Olmstead

G.K.HALL &CO.
Boston, Massachusetts
1978

Library of Congress Cataloging in Publication Data

Olmstead, Alan H
   Threshold.

   "Published in large print."
   1. Olmstead, Alan H. 2. Retirement—Biography.
I. Title.
[HQ1062.045 1977]   301.43'5   77-15470
ISBN 0-8161-6531-9

Grateful acknowledgment is made for permission to reprint an excerpt from *The Letters of Wallace Stevens* edited by Holly Stevens. Copyright © 1966 by Holly Stevens. Reprinted by permission of Alfred A. Knopf, Inc.

Published in Large Print by arrangement with Harper & Row, Publishers, Inc.

Set in Photon 18 pt Crown

To the other presence

Preface

For this kind of book, preface becomes postscript, and what the author owes his readers is an accounting of how things have been going in the interval between the days in which these entries were written and their present publication. The public record itself is adequate for the latest status of Presidents and the general welfare. In the private sector, the affirmations have been reaffirmed, and the pleasures and satisfactions have deepened; each new spring tears and builds the heart anew. Beyond that, I have had the special good fortune of being able to take this typewriter into retirement with me, and use it for an undertaking which has not only kept my spirits up but which now may also raise pleasantly complicated havoc with that retirement budget. What would I be doing with my time now if something other than the typewriter had been the tool of my trade? My uneasiness over the answer to that one, my mixed relief and regret that I haven't really had to face that degree of challenge, add to the admiration I feel for those who have been wise and resourceful enough to find their own good thing in retirement, often by the development of new skills and interests.

A.H.O.

Monday, Sept. 4, 1972. I have no job to go to tomorrow morning, and I am frightened. I know, now that this retirement moment has come, that the income won't begin to be enough. I fear for my mental outlook. I wonder if I am going to keep myself lean and busy. I am nervous over the number of people I have seen die a few months after they let go of the job routines which had been pulling them through one day after another. I have always loved my work and hated the prospect of leaving it. I have cried at some of the stages which brought this moment toward its reality. Now that the anticipation is about to be succeeded by the beginning of actual experience, I feel as if I had been sentenced to life imprisonment. But there is also a first

1

small response, in blood and brain, to the recognition that, whatever it is, it is going to be change. Either way, the fact that joblessness doesn't officially start until tomorrow gives this last authentic holiday of my life an unexpected touch of exhilaration. I make the fire and cook the meat and roast the corn in the beautiful, fateful September afternoon sunlight. The corn, having been snatched out of the ravenous chawing of this year's upsurge of woodchucks, seems especially good.

Form and Discipline

Tuesday, Sept. 5. I have firm ideas about the necessity for preserving, or perhaps creating would be more accurate, some form and discipline for this new life. One must not go slack. Therefore, I am up on time this first morning, through breakfast on time, and even have an errand — to drive to the nearest stand and buy the New York *Times,* which takes me out of the house on the old familiar time schedule. I am dressed as if for the world. When I meet a neighbor at the stand, I am brisk, alert, brighteyed, as if I were pushing out into the new day with great clarity of purpose, the perfect supply of vitality, and a serene confidence I will not be wasting my time and talent. The trouble is that, after I make such a brave show of buying the newspaper, there is no place but home to take it. I try to keep the reading functional, on the professional level at which I have read newspapers at the beginning of the day for more than forty years. The news, this morning, is of the human carnage at the Olympic Games involving the Arab commandos, the Israeli athletes, and the West German police. The first thing I realize, reading the news, is that I don't have to get myself in print inside the next few hours with my selection of deplorative adjectives or my judgment whether the police blundered. That was the compulsion that made the job tough, over all those years, until you feared there would come one morning when you could not meet the challenge. This morning I don't have to, and the truth is that I rather wish the whip was still over me, to compel me to discipline my own thinking and instinct into a line of printed words.

Is There a Life Before Death?

Wednesday, Sept. 6. As I discovered yesterday, in this, the new life — if I am going to feel able to keep on calling it a life — there is nothing out there, in the world, which really depends on me. For long years I was at least a cog; there was a place I went and a thing I did in order to keep one of the wheels turning. If I did not appear, someone else had to do something extra. I had at least this much importance to the world: that my non-appearance could create a momentary problem. Yesterday, in the first day of this new existence in which I was no longer going to a job, I disciplined myself into an imitation of a new routine. But the attempted creation of a new little world for myself did not alter or hide what was going on in that other world out there. Everything was proceeding, in what seemed its own cool heartlessness, as if I never had functioned as an integral, contributing part of society. It is as though I had been thrown into a vacuum like those created for the training of astronauts in which, while still within the world and in sight of the world, I have suddenly become weightless. Nothing out there has a reason to remember or to calculate that I exist. I should have known it could be this bad.

Things to Do

Thursday, Sept. 7. Yesterday — imagine this — I spent most of my day feeling blue over the fact that I had not been required, by the demands of an insistent, tyrannical, demanding contract of employment for pay, to produce an instant opinion on the lurid news of the Arab commando slaughter at the Olympic Games. I missed my job, and I discovered and began to resent the fact that the outside world no longer needed or expected anything from me. This made quick travesty out of one of my first resolves for this requirement caper. Pretending, with a cheery whistle and a bright, fresh-scrubbed outlook, still to be playing a meaningful, significant role in the eyes of this old world was a lost exercise. The world didn't care whether you were up early, simulating some errand through going to work traffic, or stayed in bed all day. It was yesterday, then, that I began realizing that, good as it

6

is to discipline myself into morale-sustaining routines, I need to do something more to keep some kind of ego going. Today, for quick antidote to yesterday's experience, I kept myself compulsively busy doing some of the little things that never would get done if I didn't do them. I dug out of the lawn a small protruding rock I have been mowing around, but never trimming around, for the last thirty years. I got bossy and fussy about lunch and got toast a little too dark (plus the beginning of a dark look?) for my pains. I cleaned another zone of my desk, with each throwaway severing or finalizing some kind of connection to the great outside grind. I was tired long before I ran out of things to do which meant absolutely nothing to anybody but me.

Congratulations? What For?

Friday, Sept. 8. "CONGRATULATIONS ON YOUR RETIREMENT!" What the hell for? What do people mean by this kind of sentiment? Who told the greeting card people this was not the time for CONDOLENCES? Is one to be congratulated, willy-nilly, on being too old to work? What do they know, those who seem to think it is some kind of good fortune, about the number of dollars that stand ready and organized to sustain me and mine in our way of life? It so happens that my particular situation is one in which circumstances are mixed. What happened to me was that I reached the right number of years to be eligible for retirement at the precise time a new and alien management was taking over the newspaper to which I had given my working lifetime. If I had not resigned/retired, I might conceivably have been fired. In any case, the real reason I resigned/retired was that I found it intolerable to continue working in the job I had held for thirty-one years. That was not a pleasant discovery; it was not something to be congratulated upon. The truth is that I always wanted to die with my boots on, to have "it" arrive like a stray thought or a sudden mystic insight coming in over the left shoulder — its arrival and departure, taking me with it, all in one motion, jostling the papers on my desk.

The Sea

Saturday, Sept. 9. There are times for some of us when, if we do not go to the sea, we begin to feel ourselves landlocked into a state of diminishing consciousness. The circumstances of living seem to mean less and less, the routines become negative and oppressive, the capacity for emotion desiccated. The need for some revitalizing immersion becomes obsessive; we see mirages of sunlit sand and dancing water in every landscape; finally, we rush to the shore as if to the mother of all life, to the water womb from which not only science but our own deepest intuitions show the first animation emerging. There, by surrendering and committing ourselves back to the formless ceaseless surge, we restore ourselves within our own limited shapes and purposes. Because it was long past time I went to the shore today, to a point in Rhode Island where there was nothing between me and Spain except one great uninterrupted unity of water and where this water, sparkling and brisk and clean, touched every inch of my skin with a thousand pinpoint vibrancies. Later, I became Matthew Arnold, and listened to the surf.

Even Church?

Sunday, Sept. 10. The normal American Sunday, having been crammed full of all the things there isn't time for during the working week, has become the most highly pressured day of the week. For us, the routine — some of it obligatory, some of it the result of happy inspirations — runs from the reading of somebody's letters and poetry over the breakfast coffee (this year Wallace Stevens on both counts) through the Sunday papers and then out of doors toward some open-air project for which only weekends offer enough time, with, somewhere along the route, the nap without which a Sunday would not be a Sunday. All these routines have worked themselves, over the years, into the status of seventh day necessities. There has never been time, therefore, for a run out on the highways, a casual drop-in on some friend to see what kind of Sunday prison he has built for himself, for a Sunday afternoon concert, or a neighborhood movie, or for

11

the improvisation of something I just wanted to do. Today, the first retirement Sunday, has been exactly like every other Sunday except that it has included the beginning of rebellious thoughts. Some of these activities which have taken over Sunday because there was no time for them on any other day can now, if I really please, *be put off* to some other day of the week. I may be able, now, to find a way to do on Sunday something I would really like to do on a Sunday. Perhaps Sunday has been liberated. It occurs to me: I might even, some Sunday, be able, have time, to go to church.

Should Retired People Change Houses?

Monday, Sept. 11. When we came to this house, the wide boards in the floors had been covered with layers of green or maroon floor paint. We sanded them off, down to the clear grain, and then stewed butternut husks, from the tree at the edge of the yard, until we had a brew dark enough to use to stain the floors. This we did ourselves. The maple tree that stands outside the kitchen window, now fifty feet tall, is one four of us carried half a mile down from the hill. We didn't believe so large a sapling could be transplanted successfully, but it lived for us. Although we seldom taste the fruit, we planted the russet apple trees by the garage. The black oak in the middle of the lawn provided the canopy for A's wedding ceremony, an August afternoon's midsummer dream of an affair. In our early winters here, it was around the fireplace just to the right of this desk that we gathered for such mid-Victorian family rituals as the reading aloud of *David Copperfield* and *Mary Poppins.* This is the house of our Christmases and our Thanksgivings, the house to which our children came home, with new friends, from their first semesters in college, the house which could open out for our good times and provide suffering corners for our moments of pain. It is also, of course, the house which is beginning to need to be shingled again, even though we told ourselves, when we selected expensive wood shingles thirteen years ago, that that was probably the last roof we would have to pay for. Its vast outer surface will soon be asking for fresh paint. Its interior pipes grow porous; the cost of heat escalates every winter; there really is no hard-boiled statistical way of proving that we can afford to stay here and keep the place livable. But move into something smaller and less expensive and easier to maintain? Only, in present mood, as a dead body.

I Have to Live
With Myself

Tuesday, Sept. 12. C noticed that my day had begun with a shower, and recalled, accurately, that this had been happening every retirement morning. It is true that, as against erratic habits during the work years, I have been taking a shower every morning, needed or not. I don't, as yet, really enjoy the process except when it comes to the final result, which is one of feeling especially well conditioned to face the world. But here, of course, is the curious part. I am no longer facing the world. After so sanitizing myself that I would not need to fear the most intimate kind of office cooperation, even on a hot day in a non-air-conditioned office, I am spending my time away from people, potentially odorant to nobody, the Ivory gleam on my pate visible to nobody except the mailman if he should be looking back. So that was C's question: Why Mr. So-Clean now, instead of back when I was out among people all day? The answer came so glibly I myself wasn't aware, at first, just how logical and important it was. "Because," I told her, "now I have to live with myself." This may be the most significant by far of all the discoveries I can make about the retirement state. I have to live with myself. No more alibis that may be good enough for somebody else. No more standards more compelling than my own. No more compromises supposedly justified just because I am so busy. I have to live with myself. How often, I wonder, am I going to encounter that, as a mandate?

What to Save for a Rainy Day

Wednesday, Sept. 13. Folklore suggests unpleasant associations for rainy days, making them something one ought to save money for, but that is not the way people remember them. The first thing a rainy day meant to me was a happy, even if enforced, cloistering with dolls, blocks and books on the porch at the farm; my cousins and I pretended we wished it would stop raining so we could do something else. Next, there were those summer afternoons, musty with hints of forbidden knowledge and forbidden practices, which we children spent hiding out in a deep corner of the hay mow. Later on, by a few years, a day that was too wet for work in the fields could be ruled, by the magnificent alchemy of logic Uncle Ed could invoke, a day when he and I should go fishing, where it didn't matter how wet we got. The next rain I remember — encountered many years later, perhaps suitably enough during a rainy afternoon's reading in a high room in Harkness Quadrangle — was the rain that Edwin Arlington Robinson made come down all one day, a symbol of temporary peace and security around the castle where he had brought his lovers Tristram and Isolt fast together. A quarter century later I was on a farm again, and it rained all one October Sunday which I spent in the corn crib, shelling the season's ears. A few more years, and there was a rainy day at the Cape, and I lay in a state of perfect rest until, in the afternoon, the rain became too beautiful not to walk in, along Nauset Beach. Always, a rainy day has been a kind of special blessing, a release from other responsibilities and linkages into a benevolent luxury license all its own. Today has been a rainy day, and I have been reading, and sitting on the porch watching the rain fall, and walking into it to get vegetables from the garden, and spending this much of it remembering. The thing to save up for a rainy day is yourself.

The Blue Ribbon

Thursday, Sept. 14. One hoes and trenches and weeds and weeds and waters all spring and summer and hopes to have a product worthy of being taken, in imagination at least, to the fair. Lurking down deep inside every gardener, however brusque his pretense that he seeks merely such practical returns as personal therapy or the best food for the family table, there is this recurrent dream of the perfect display, taking Grange blue ribbons. Once in a generation, perhaps, there comes a whole garden that might stand for such judging. But in most years variations in weather and pestilence and in the sweat and skill of the gardener himself produce mixed results, and the gardener welcomes any fortuitous opportunity to make a selective display of his product. Today we were to visit some elderly pensioners (we the young pensioners?) for whom casual gifts of sustenance would be appropriate. I found, close to the heart of the sprawling tomato vines, a collection of some fifteen fruit, uniform in size, beautifully ruddy in color and wonderfully solid-looking. By this time of the season our burpless cucumbers had begun to deviate into unsightly twists and bulges, but I still managed to find four that were long and regular and slim, as in mid-August. I selected two great round Spanish onions, and four medium-size look-alike peppers, and, as a real delicacy, a cellophane bag full of green snap beans, all long and straight and at the precise size that combines the ultimate in crispness with a good fullness of flavor. To this collection, arranged in tomato red and varied greens, C added a harvest of September rosebuds. There were, when the display was delivered, some appropriate remarks from the recipients, who professed to be vastly pleased and impressed. But by this time, to tell the truth, we had already awarded ourselves the big blue ribbon and filed that deserved triumph away and begun our first thinking about gardening next year.

The Places Poets Find

Friday, Sept. 15. Robert Frost picked, for his final country home in Ripton, Vermont, a spot that combined both of the features he seems to have had in mind all his home-hunting life. The house was high up and near the crest of a great, eastward-facing hill. And it was at the high end of a dead-end road. In his two previous Vermont choices, down in South Shaftsbury, back in the days when he himself still had illusions he was a working farmer, he had been forced to settle for less — his first farm on a hill, but also on a main road; his second secure with its own dead-end road, but without a hill. But at Ripton he obtained that combination of height and privacy which poets seem to have an extraordinary success in finding. Down in Cornwall,

21

Connecticut, Mark Van Doren located himself halfway up a hillside, at the end of a road which led only to his place. Midway between Van Doren territory and Frost territory Archibald MacLeish, in Conway, Massachusetts, lives at the summit of a hill high enough to give him naked-eye looks into New Hampshire and, although his road is not dead end, it has that atmosphere, in that when you get to the MacLeish place, you cannot see any other house in any direction. We have, over the years, paid surreptitious, unannounced homage calls on all these locations without disturbing their peace. Today we were making a second visit to the Frost grave in Bennington Cemetery, another spot Frost selected, high on a hill, last stop on a road that led no farther.

The Lure of the Track

Saturday, Sept. 16. Back in August I went out of my way to arrange a day at the track. It was intended, in view of the way I was looking forward into my retirement finances, to be my farewell to the horses. Today, I have been to the track again. When the expedition was suggested, I could not poor-mouth a refusal; it somehow seemed imperative to pretend that I still had enough money and enough spirit to risk a day of manly pleasure. Once again I learned, as I do almost every time, that the race track is that unique place in the world where the wonderfully exciting anticipation of arriving and getting the first bet down is most swiftly succeeded by a dejected willingness to leave. But always, against that, there is the renewed experience of that moment when, at the head of the stretch, one is suddenly, miraculously in contention. This is a moment which, for its grip on all one's senses and viscera, is

23

unparalleled in human experience and cannot be bought or staged anywhere else. In the obstinate, unreasonable search for such moments one is clinging to the possibility that life itself can be rich and robust. The other day I noticed two busloads of local Golden Agers leaving town early in the morning, and later I heard that they had gone to the track that day and that three of them had hit the daily double. This brings me to the disclosure that C, who doesn't even want to go to the track or traffic in its kind of thrill, had the double for $65.80 today. Some people have all the urge and others have all the luck.

The Big Deadline

Sunday, Sept. 17. All one's working life is aimed at one deadline or another — the job that has to be done by noon, or by the time to go home, or by the end of the week. This continual series of small deadlines is what keeps people and the world going thoughtlessly and, on the whole, contentedly along in a kind of self-renewing drudgery. Now, in this retirement, most of the little deadlines have gone out of one's life. No one has to have this or that detail disposed of by a certain hour, day, or week. But all these little deadlines of the past, as they have faded, have been succeeded by one big new deadline — something like the sudden-death period in sports, when every play or stroke may be the last, the one that determines the final score of the whole long game. There is, for the senior citizen, only so much time left for *everything,* for all of it added together. Where there were once various enterprises that needed to be completed on schedule, the new big deadline is one against which all one's life must necessarily be completed. None of the petty exigencies matters much any more. But what one really wants to do before the big deadline arrives — that is what it is urgently important to find out, and to do, if one can.

An Escape From Football?

Monday, Sept. 18. Yesterday was the first Sunday of the new football season. It was also a critical day in the American League divisional race, with the Red Sox, Orioles, Tigers, and Yankees all bunched within a game and a half of one another. Normally, with a new shuffle of football Giants opening their season, and Namath pitching for the Jets, I would be with the football networks from the one o'clock beginning, shuttling between them, and possibly running a roving radio on the baseball games at the same time. This would have been one of those dream Sundays, in which a man makes exaggerated claim of his right to choose a man's world. During those months when I

26

was trying to imagine what retirement life would be like, Sunday football was always one of the reassuring pluses that would account for at least one big block of time. Yesterday, however, I behaved with a strange indifference to my opportunity for a big sports Sunday. At one o'clock I was out in the yard, getting ready to mow the lawn. After a stint of lawn I pruned a section of hedge. A little after four o'clock, I caught the last eight minutes of the Giants game, and then, later, switching networks, a few minutes of the first half of the Miami-Kansas City swelter in a hundred degrees at Kansas City. I didn't bother with the second half, and didn't know the ball scores until going-to-sleep radio time. Have I changed? Is retirement going to develop other surprise twists in my habits and diversions? Was I merely adjusting to the fact that I wouldn't be at any office this morning for the usual Monday morning quarterbacking? Or have I, by some miracle, come to at least momentary terms with myself so that I no longer feel the need to escape from myself into a world of make-believe that tries to make itself real by crushing bones?

From the Terrace, Live

Tuesday, Sept. 19. Red Smith, in the New York *Times* yesterday, wrote a column titled "The Sabbath, an Electronic Rhapsody," in which he recounted his faithful monitoring of the television and radio sports bonanza Sunday. He watched and heard the same games I would normally have followed, and, reading him, I got it all in ten minutes. Perhaps I'll let Smith do it for me more often, at least until we come to the dread season of the holidays, when the pretended necessity of watching some game is the rude male excuse for not joining the togetherness crunch in the parlor. As for all the perfunctory viewing I might have done Sunday, the very thought of such second-rate, media-filtered entertainment was put to shame, during yesterday's breakfast on the terrace, by an intense, live, in the flesh and feather period of bird activity. It was bird breakfast time, too, on pokeberry, dogwood fruit, weed seeds, and on insects apparently being found on every leaf, branch, and stem. A female grosbeak tumbled down a weed; goldfinches looped the loop; the rich brown of a thrasher flashed across the lawn and into the center of the dogwood tree; cool, competent catbirds sat by, waiting in vain to hear anything to imitate. The truth was, the birds were so busy they were — except for the occasional whistle-mutter of the starlings — very quiet. As always, there were nondescript small birds we could not identify, even with C on the glasses. For the fifteen years or so in which we have been bird conscious, I have always sworn that the ideal morning would be one when, if the birds began a period of activity like this, I could sit there as long as I pleased until one of these perpetual strangers should hit the right pose in the right slant of sun and become known to us. Yesterday morning, after twenty minutes of it, and with no job to go to, I nevertheless got up and went into the house. It seems I would rather write about a potential morning of bird watching than do it. If we really wanted to do any of the things we have always told ourselves we wanted to do, the moment we had time, we would have done them long ago, by making time for them.

Short Honeymoon?

Wednesday, Sept. 20. I felt frightened and uneasy about this condition of life before I entered it, and today, the sixteenth day of the new life (or slow death), that was the way it was again. In the meantime, I have been on a honeymoon with the retirement idea. I have been seducing myself into pretending that I have been seeing some aspects of life as if for the first time. There has been a dream of a world that is a marvelous and hitherto unknown delight and opportunity, now suddenly wide open to the most fantastic desires. This has been an adventure, with expectation of something new and different every day, and so far there has been at least something, some piece of mail, some encounter, some possibility of a future activity, that has helped foster the illusion that the exit from the old world has freed me into a golden opportunity really to live, at last. Today, like all human moods, whatever their direction, the euphoria began to wear off. It may be — rather, it almost has to be — that instead of the great opening of new excitements, this is really the beginning of a settled, stable and ultimately monotonous condition in which nothing is ever going to change very much, certainly not for the better. This world which momentarily seemed so fresh and stimulating and blessedly busy was that way merely because a drastic change in condition and routine stimulated my physiological and psychological resources to abnormal response. Before I come down with a cold there is always a half day when I feel an exceptionally high body tone. The blood cells detect the infection before I do and launch a counterattack which makes me feel deceptively well just before I find out that I am sick. Today I have been listless, uneasy about how the pattern of this new life is really going to establish itself, and uncertain whether there is stuff enough left inside me to deal with it on even terms.

Retirement Arithmetic

Thursday, Sept. 21. Some others may be more interested in the financial specifics of this adventure than I am. Here, if they want to play around with my problem, is the situation. I have $6,800 in the savings account. I began scraping it together the day the new ownership walked in the door last November, which was when I realized I would either want to, or have to, leave my job sooner or later. I have, at today's quotations, about four thousand dollars in nine stocks. That, outside of the land, which may or may not find some kind of buyer soon, represents capital assets. As for income, I have not yet seen the first checks of my new status. Social Security will be something like $258 for me, $110 for C. The pension from the paper will be something like $140. The only actual earning I am still doing, selling the tri-weekly column to five newspapers, brings in twenty-four dollars a week. All this adds up, with chances of an occasional television panel job thrown in, to something like seven thousand dollars a year, as compared to the sixteen thousand it used to take to keep this establishment going. The first big slice that has to come out of that seven thousand is one of fourteen hundred dollars for town taxes. The second big hit is going to be for the heating bill for this big, drafty, nonretirement house. I have never really dared, especially when thinking about retirement, to add up the oil bills for a year. But they must go close to one thousand dollars. So taxes and heat alone will be taking nearly twenty-five hundred dollars out of the seven thousand, leaving a grand total of forty-five hundred for everything else. Somebody more finance-minded than I could calculate his prospects realistically in advance. I am going to find out how I make out by the experience, and I am prepared to take a year avoiding the answer. What I stand to get in the way of a life is, I am sure, better than nothing. The question is, in human terms, for me, and for everybody who retires without capital resource of his own, how much better than nothing.

Money

Friday, Sept. 22. As may have been judged from yesterday's entry, a proper reverence and care for money is as impossibly difficult for some of us retirees, now we need to have it so desperately, as it was during all the years of supposed opportunity in which we so carelessly neglected to make ourselves rich. It has been my own fortune, or misfortune, to have a special trauma about money, which dates from the most distasteful experience of my young life. I had just won my scholarship to Yale, and the distinguished scholarship fund trustees who had selected me felt some touch of responsibility for guiding my future. One of these trustees was a bank director, and his idea of how to fire me up with ambition and thirst for success was to take me down into the bank vault and there place a small packet of thousand-dollar bills in my hand and inform me that that was a million dollars, and how did it

35

feel to have a million dollars in my hand? The answer might have been dictated by the fact that I was wearing, at that moment, an ill-fitting, shoddy eighteen-dollar suit. But instead of feeling hunger for crisp bills of large denominations, instead of making an instant resolve for a Horatio Alger career which would lead me back into that vault in my own right, I felt frightened and nervous and unhappy, and these same feelings have flooded over me ever since, every time there has been a moment when it seemed I might be beginning to have enough money in hand to represent real security. It is not that I do not love money. The accumulation of it is the poison my whole system rejects. And if there had been any conceivable way I could have ended up having less resource for these retirement years, I would have been sure to find it and take it. Even now, when I supposedly know that what I have and get is all there is, and that I have to make it do, I am not interested. The only pleasant, peaceful feeling I get from money is when money is in motion, in ebb and flow. Whether it would have been otherwise if I had never had that million-dollar packet thrust into my hand I will never know, but I have always felt grateful to that bank director for a result he did not intend. What a horrible thing it would have been to spend a lifetime in worship of the stuff!

No More Vacations

Saturday, Sept. 23. This has for many years been the time in September when we would be taking off for our vacation. The twin annual compulsions — to get away from the desk, to be close to the sound and wet and smell of salt water — combined with one more annual urgency, to get C away from the stove and the sink, would always take charge of us sometime during the last ten days of the month and send us forth, usually to the Cape. The short vacation that would follow would be plush and expensive. This year, in the new status, there are fewer compulsions. There is no tyrant desk to get away from. It seems a little pleasant to be home in September. Still, there is something sad and final in saying farewell to that well-earned self-indulgence in which, when we did take a few days, we took them first class, paying something like seventy dollars a day for having everything available on a platter. We will, in the new kind of life, be going away for a night or two. But, although many other experiences in this new life have turned out to be different from our expectation, we really do not expect the shortened expedition, when we take it, to be quite so much leisure, so much change, so much fun. Still, we would calculate that we are better off classifying ourselves among the retired poor rather than the retired rich, for whom moving about from one vacation-style existence to another so often becomes the most demanding and insistent kind of occupation. A true vacation has to be *from* something.

One Passage From
Wallace Stevens
I Possibly Understand

Sunday, Sept. 24. Every Sunday morning, after breakfast, C reads some of Wallace Stevens's letters and one or two of his poems. We like the letters for their glimpses into the way this amazing character combined the career of Hartford insurance executive with that of successful poet. Reading the poems is, for us, a weekly exercise in intellectual humility. What we don't understand fills the volume. But what brings Stevens here, in these notes, is the fact that in one of the letters C read this morning, written a few days after he had had his seventy-third Christmas, and the morning after a ''really winter weekend,'' the poet-executive seemed to be dealing with symptoms in his life to which there may be developing parallels in my own current experience. During the weekend snow, sleet, and rain, Stevens wrote, "I wanted to stay in bed and make for myself a weekend world far more extraordinary than the one that most people make for themselves. But the habitual, customary, has become, at my age, such a pleasure in itself that it is coming to be that that pleasure is at least as great as any. It is a large part of the normality of the normal. And, I suppose, that projecting this idea to its ultimate extension, the time will arrive when just to *be* will take in everything without the least *doing* since even the least doing is irrelevant to pure being. When the time comes when just to be does in fact take in everything, I may just do my being on the banks of the Rio Yayabo. You will already have observed the abstract state of my mind. This is in part due to the fact that I have done little or no reading, little or no writing or walking or thinking. I have not been to New York. In short, I have been working at the office, nothing else: complaining a little about it but content, after all, that I have that solid rock under my feet.''

That is what C read this morning to me, another aging individual who, by contrast, has had no special world created by his own genius, who no longer has any solid rock job in the regular world, but who, nevertheless, begins to feel the lazy siren lure of just to be without doing anything.

The Last of the Lark

Monday, Sept. 25. For a fixed-income retirement, the economic arguments against a second car are conclusive, even when the second car is a beloved veteran family institution. To carry insurance on the Lark costs something like $125 a year. Registration costs fifteen dollars. Taxes are, after twelve years of book devaluation, down to almost nothing. But there is a big dollar trap inside every such ancient vehicle; any next thing that goes wrong is likely to drive the garagemen into that experimental replacement of parts which sometimes can go on and on without hitting any real cure for trouble which, realistically, ought to be accepted as a terminal condition the moment the first symptom appears. The only argument which could justify a modest retirement family in retaining two cars would be one of sheer logistical necessity. But, in the new life we are leading, there is not likely to be any situation in which both of us absolutely have to be in different places at the same time. So today the Lark went to the junkyard where, in honor of the fact that it had arrived under its own power, the automotive undertaker agreed to take it without charging anything for his rites. This, for us, was the common sense thing to do. But no one should think it was as easy as this accounting may have made it seem. This Lark was the last automobile built with floors flush with its doors and with headroom enough so that one could wear a hat without bumping it, high enough so one could enter or exit the rear seat standing and with leg room enough so that one could stretch out forward in the rear seat. It says something about how we take care of ourselves that the most sensible, comfortable, roomy automobile of the post-war generation should fail to make a market life for itself. Henceforth I am condemned to the stoop-and-twist system for getting into a car. The Lark had room. It had grace and style, like a dignified modest relative to the aristocratic Mercedes. It had economy. It was a beautiful automobile.

Are Retired Husbands in the Way?

Tuesday, Sept. 26. The standard question asked of the wife in a retiring couple is "What's it going to be like, having him around the house?'' It is probably one of the first questions she asks herself. Now that we have been in the new state for nearly a month, C is still being asked the same question. Her responses are always somehow kept away from me. The only thing she has said to me directly is that it makes it difficult for her to find a right time for vacuuming, since she knows the house-filling sound annoys me. It has to go into the record, however, that when I did return from a sortie we both knew would take a couple of hours, it was the telephone, not the vacuum cleaner, I found in operation. But it was another telephone call she received today, while I was here, that made me wonder. The call came before I was through with my morning work stint. It lasted only a moment; C ran upstairs and ten minutes later came down all dressed to go out, a modern-day speed record for her. She had, she said, been invited to go see a garden. Then she was out of the house and gone, with not a solicitous thought for my welfare. When she came back three hours later, she seemed buoyant, as if she had accomplished something more than visit a garden. Come to think of it, she has been going out more, on sudden impulses, and on slight errands, as if, perhaps, she thought she needed to escape from the house and/or me. I must try to draw her out on this some day. This house ought to be big enough for two people.

Do It in September

Wednesday, Sept. 27. If these words are reaching anybody who has not yet made his entrance into this final threshold, this last beginning, let me recommend that he do it in September. There are certain to be, set like soft precious stones into gold, a number of days that go well with the moods of the retirement act and state. This morning there were mists that enclosed breakfast on the terrace in a friendly seclusion, shrouding the known workaday world of the past from view, but opening up overhead to a patch of blue sky traversed by sea-fern clouds, each a new shape never precisely so fashioned before, on a journey never charted before. This afternoon the sun was warm enough to invite dozeful sitting on the lawn, but bright clean air imparted that blessed initiative which gets up from indolent comfort to enjoy the even greater luxury of accomplishing some bothersome task long postponed. The mixture of repose and energy, of benediction and challenge, of summary and prospectus which is to be found in the airs and fields and suns of September forms a bridge between two states of living. There is, on one hand, the sweet, sere sadness of complete things, not to be grown or lived again on or in the same stalk — and in this, September is the month of the aging. But so compulsive is the thought of the things fading, and the beauty of what was or what might have been — so good does life seem in this forced seasonal retrospect — that one somehow feels in creaking bones and tired flesh a piratical urge to seize yet a little more of life's precious booty before calling it a day, a month, or a life. September is the month which provides the mood and setting for letting some things draw to a close, and then, in the nick of time, for taking a new and perhaps altered grip on sensations one cannot and ought not let go. The combination could be what retirement is all about.

Does Micawber Learn to Pinch Pennies?

Thursday, Sept. 28. If, in your Micawberish way, you paid no proper attention to pennies during the years of your earning power, a proper regard for the admonitions of society, as well as for your own dubious conscience, now demands that you go at least one round of penny-pinching penance. This we have now done. To be able to conduct our experiment dispassionately we selected cat food, an item in the weekly food budget that does not concern our own appetites or digestive systems. At first it looked as if we scored a complete and early triumph. We had developed a habit of buying a weekly bag of cat food along with our Sunday papers. Now, for the first time, we noticed the price, which was $1.19. The next step was comparison shopping. On our next trip to the supermarket we bought the same bag, same size, same brand, for $1.09. Ten cents a week, fifty-two weeks a year, amounted to $5.20. The lesson, and the future procedure, were obvious. The next week, however, the supermarket shelf was bare of that particular brand. We went to another supermarket and it was also out of it. We bought another brand the cats, it developed, didn't like. The next week the only thing we could find on supermarket shelves was our original brand in smaller size boxes, the tariff for five pounds adding up to $1.24, or more than the $1.19 we had been paying at the fruit stand where we get our Sunday papers. Every Sunday, incidentally, the fruit stand, where we could be making our weekly purchase peacefully without any extra expense for gasoline driving from one supermarket to another, has been well stocked with the bag we used to buy. Meanwhile, cat food, instead of being a routine thing, has become a special worry, until we almost seem to be letting our entire shopping week revolve around it. We could, of course, take on more cats, and thus increase the amount we can save each year by our industrious comparison shopping. At this point, however, we let our experiment stand, for all those interested in a serious analysis of retirement economics. To them, also, we relinquish, for a time at least, all our own claim and interest in any other marvelous ways for retirement couples to begin a belated pinching of pennies.

The Gentle Errands

Friday, Sept. 29. For years we had been noticing a retired couple who, although they couldn't possibly have anything very important to do, always seemed to be heading toward some particular place, wearing an atmosphere of definite, though unhurried, purpose. We marveled how, at their age — an eminence we in those days never really conceived of as something also drawing nearer for ourselves — they kept themselves moving about and active, just as if some consequence were involved. This afternoon we found out about it for ourselves. It was easy! Because she could not seem to find what she wanted in this town's stores, I volunteered to drive C across the river and through the interchanges to the shopping mecca favored by the elite. When the elite went to this area of the finer shops, they usually met to eat in a certain restaurant. It was time for me, after hearing about it for all these years, to see it for myself. I ordered what looked to be the most masculine item on the menu — a hot turkey sandwich. It proved to be a slice of sparrow delicately coated with spray-on gravy on a thin single slice of bread. After lunch we separated, C to look for a sweater and I to pay a surprise call on an erstwhile professional friend whom I had never had time to visit in his own office. He was out, for the longer lunch people who still have jobs can afford. Back at the car C had not found her sweater and now wished to go back to our own town and buy, after all, one she had seen there. We made our slow, passive way through the heavy afternoon shift traffic, stopped downtown, and arrived home, nothing consequential accomplished. An afternoon of leisurely moving about, all dressed up and doing something together, had somehow proved capable of generating a gentle, intoxicating kind of fun. A retired couple going about its non-business is not necessarily a pair of sad, closed-out losers.

Audit to Date

Saturday, Sept. 30. At the end of the first month, a performance audit:

Getting out of bed time: Average loss of ten minutes from the old rigid going-to-work routine of 6:30. Worst threat: A potentially poisonous habit of realizing I do not really have to get up.

Getting dressed up: So far, coat and tie every single weekday morning. It feels good for itself, and lends additional luxuriousness to the afternoon splendor of just a pair of shorts out around the lawn.

Missing the old job: I am more inclined to ask why I didn't do this long ago.

Keeping busy: No problem. Finding time seems to be.

The pills: The fear they would become a crutch has not materialized. I am taking few now and feeling no worse physically. But so far, to be cautiously honest, no boredom such as sometimes drives people to take pills in order to have something important to do.

Weight: Beautiful! I have no idea why, but I'm down ten pounds since I stopped working.

Finances: So far, no bad breaks.

Accomplishment: What was the score for the first sixty-five years?

Once More, a Sunday Walk

Sunday, Oct. 1. I was peacefully hacking my way through some brush, opening a path toward our stand of Christmas trees, when Dr. T. came after me in the wilderness. Proclaiming that I apparently had nothing else really important to do, he insisted I accompany him in a walk up the road to an antique auto show and flea market. I have little interest in antique autos, and none in flea markets, and had always successfully ignored both. But Dr. T. put on a special insistence, as if he had a right to proclaim that I had nothing more important to do and a right to prescribe, indeed, that such an impromptu turn among exotic motors and the odd buffs who cared about them, would be good for my health. To please him — only to please him — I went with him. We found, among the buffs, another friend; it was a pleasant saunter, in the afternoon sun, down the lines of ancient motors; some recalled the first automobiles I had ridden in and driven, a half century before. They didn't have my Maxwell, or Jack Benny's either; they did have exactly the same Lincoln I had driven in 1926, only it looked unbelievably snub-nosed in contrast to my memory of magnificent and massive power. The show was more unpressured fun than I would have guessed; doing something like this, at an easy pace, in the easy undemanding company of a male friend or two did seem, after all, to be the kind of thing one could afford to do in a retirement status. A half century ago, on a Sunday afternoon, a man would go down the road and look in on a neighbor and perhaps take him on a walk, which was a nice thing to do on a Sunday afternoon. This was the first time, since college days when a fledgling Dwight Macdonald would drop by and lead me on a walk through the snows of the Whitney Avenue reservoir, that I had had any similar experience. And after all, it was true that I really had nothing else I had to do.

That Old Monday Surge

Monday, Oct. 2. It is time to unmask some of the folklore lies about Monday, which is supposed to be the day everybody hates and dreads because it is so hard to get back into the work groove. Even when I had a job groove to get back into, Mondays weren't that way for me. Instead of being blue, they were likely to be unusually cheerful, which was my own response to the change from the weekend world of "what shall we do" back to the world of something "that has to be done." My spirit sang, rather than wilted, in the process of rejoining what was, apparently, the good old grind. More than this, Monday had come to be my most productive day. Instead of finding it difficult to face the desk every Monday morning, I began the new week with sure, speedy fingers on the typewriter, and with a crisp willingness to try decisions which, on another day, might seem forbiddingly difficult. What I now discover is that this Monday impulse has, so far, been carried over into this new existence. I am still such a powerhouse on Monday that I am likely, if I don't watch out, to rip off all the lighter work quota of a semi-retirement week and then come to days, toward the end of the week, when I have no work rib to hold me together. It is still rosy Monday, raring to go. I may be some kind of oddball. Or does everybody, underneath the ritualistic grumbling, really feel the same way about Monday? Has that folklore Monday really disappeared, along with wash day?

When Good Pensioners Get Together

Tuesday, Oct. 3. We went down to the shore to spend the day with good friends who entered the retirement state a year ago. It was pleasant to see them and pleasant to talk to them, especially after we had finally disposed of the inevitable business of telling each other what it was like to be "free." That part of the day was the kind of disappointment, the risk of mutual downgrading that good friends should go to great lengths to spare each other. Peter claimed to have had, and still to be having, after his year, all those "insightful" reactions to the new state that I have been discovering in my first month and was so eager to pass on to him. All these new realizations and perceptions — like the unexpected "busyness" of the retirement day, or the more solemn discovery that living and dying have now, for us, been united into one process — which seemed to establish me as a very sentient kind of fellow when I was exclaiming over them to myself, and in this diary, are also his. It is possible, of course, that Peter is also a one in a million, very unusual gentleman, a very perceptive observer, with finely tuned sensitivities, who is also exceptionally brilliant in the business of mining his own experience. But suppose neither of us is that special. Suppose what seems novel and surprising to us is also the experience, novel and surprising to them also, to be sure, of all pensioners? In that case, pensioners would do a kindness to one another to stop exchanging the same wonderful discoveries about their state and go fishing, as Peter and I almost did, and should have.

Who Answers the Telephone?

Wednesday, Oct. 4. The rule I made is this: When the telephone rings, I will always wait for C to answer it. The chances are overwhelming that it will be for her. If the call is for me, she will ask who it is, and then summon me. There are certain advantages to such a system:

1. I don't have to explain to people who ought to know anyway why I am at home and not working any more.

2. I don't have to make up amiable chit-chat for people who just want to talk to C.

3. I don't have to keep needlessly invading C's privacy. I can ask her, after she has hung up, who it was and what he or she wanted.

4. I achieve an atmosphere of aloofness and importance, as if C were my secretary.

At first, this system worked beautifully. What with left-over bits and ends of business from the office, with solicitous calls from people wishing me well in the new estate, and with tantalizingly tentative suggestions of potential new activities for great gain, there were three calls for me to every one for C, and both of us had to be near the phone all the time, C to answer it and I to take over. Lately, the pattern has changed. The phone seems to have forgotten it is for us both. For C, business seems to be increasing, as if her friends, playing it cool and aloof in the first days they knew I might be around the house, were relaxing again, and she with them. The conversations are getting longer, taking the instrument out of commission for long periods during which somebody might, after all, be trying desperately to reach me. There are times when, busy as I am with important tasks of my own, an occasional break in the routine might be possible. Perhaps it wouldn't be a bad idea, if I happen to be near the phone when it rings, to do a little answering for myself.

Somebody Wants Me

Thursday, Oct. 5. Is there any way to convey to a younger reader, or to anybody still reasonably secure in his own functional place in society, just what it means to a man of sixty-five, his career brought to an end by unpleasant compulsions, to discover that he is still wanted for the competence he spent more than forty years developing? That he is still considered a sound investment? That what he may be able to perform, although it may be for only a short span of time, is considered good enough to outbalance the risks involved in making the scene for it? The discovery, if it comes to that man of sixty-five, is the gift of oxygen, of hope, of self-respect. It is a great, magnanimous deliverance from the worst of all human fears — the terribly common, but no less terrible, fear of not being wanted. Today the piece of a job I might eventually have gone looking for has come looking for me. It fits neatly, money-wise, into the Social Security pattern. All I have to do is say yes, and it begins. I do say yes, really without thinking very much about it. Two months ago I would have considered the connection involved a little shabby, and would have thrown the possibility abruptly out of my mind. Today I am much less proud and much more nakedly human. It is not the right amount of money, rather easily earned, that persuades me. It is that I have to grab at the demonstrable fact that somebody wants me as if it were all of life, which it is.

Should One Help
With the Dishes?

Friday, Oct. 6. Between the dessert and the evening television there now hovers an insidious unspoken suggestion which has not been present in our home since the earliest and most naïve days of our marriage. Back then, it was a delight to do anything that meant being close to one another. In our maturity, there has been a tacit understanding that the good life together depends on occasional divergences of activity. A good example of the way this understanding has worked out over the years would be this: after supper, when C goes back into the kitchen, I go to the television. Now, in the new state, there is a subtle, pleading uncertainty — in my mind at least — in that moment of getting up from the table. The uncertain suggestion hovering there, in that moment, is this: since I no longer go out and drudge all day in an office in order to bring home the bacon, perhaps it

64

has now come time for me to lighten the work load C has been carrying at home all these years. So almost any evening, now, there comes that fleeting moment when I almost ask whether I shouldn't come out and "dry tonight." I know that, if I make the suggestion, the answer will be a reassuring and robust "No, I don't want you out there," or "No, I like to do the dishes by myself." But what if I should make the suggestion again the next evening, and the next? Or what if, instead of talking about it, I should just go out and grab a towel and then a dish? Do I really want to put the issue to that kind of test? Perhaps, if I keep on doing nothing, minding my own business, that hovering suggestion will go away, and I will once more be able to get up from the dining-room table and walk toward the television couch without corner-eyeing C to see if I detect the slightest flicker, anywhere in her expression, of an awareness that the very mature, like the newlyweds, might also do dishes together.

I Do Dry the Dishes

Saturday, Oct. 7. One of the clear and ever present dangers of this retirement state is that there is no longer much of a buffer between thought and action, impulse and performance, suggestion and compliance. The other day Dr. T. came into the yard and suggested a walk up the road and I, with remarkably weak resistance, turned my whole Sunday around, rather enjoyably. When I think of doing something, the mere thought may become a commitment trap. Yesterday, in this space, I was trying to examine, with some objectivity, the question of whether or not, after supper, I should begin going out into the kitchen rather than to the television. That was only yesterday. Tonight I took the very same entangling kind of test action I had warned myself against yesterday. I went out into the kitchen and ostentatiously grabbed a towel, then a dish. My worst premonitions were realized immediately. Instead of turning on me with that firm resolution of hers and reminding me how she really likes to do the dishes alone, C leaned toward me and against my shoulder softly, and then, in coy encouragement and invitation, hot-sprayed the next dish in the rack. "Be careful," she said, in one of those moments of deep, meaningful communication that bless really fortunate marriages, "it will be real hot." Tonight, being there at her side felt better than being in with the television. But I must try to discipline myself. It doesn't have to be a regular thing.

Sermon

Sunday, Oct. 8. With the brain part of me, I can buy the theory that this is all a business of chance — and of deterministic chance at that. But I can't make myself feel that way, and I have no intention of living a single minute of my share of time that way. There is, for me, no compelling necessity to try to resolve the conflict between brain-science and emotion-intuition; let that be the business of those who, from the beginning, have made a profession of being the questioner-philosophers of this human story. For the rest of us, it need make no difference why we are here; we cannot alter or control the why of it, even if we think we discover it. But while we are here, we may have — I say may have because I cannot shut out the deterministic theories — the privilege of selecting a style of life for ourselves. Let me put this on the totally safe side, and concede that what I am about to say may be merely the inevitable result of the particular mixture of chromosomes, chemicals, and environment which has gone into the fashioning of "me." This, then, could be what it has been decreed I shall say at this moment, on this theme: No matter why we are here, there is a possibility we have a chance to fashion ourselves a certain life-style; the closer this comes to avoiding injury to others or to ourselves, the closer it comes to evoking the better part of others or ourselves, the closer it comes to a decent handling of whatever talents and opportunities and friendships and loves have been within our reach, the better. If, beyond this, we find heart and energy to push out against injustice, to refuse even our passive complicity to violence of any kind, mental or physical, even better. The line we draw across our millimetric time-space sector may be scuffed out the moment we leave it. But we ought to feel pretty passionate about trying to make it, up to that point, as fine and, if we are terribly lucky, as beautiful a line as we can.

Act of Emancipation

Monday, Oct. 9. For twenty years I have been waiting to do this. During all that time, the western section of our lawn has been the part I hated most to mow. It had a petty torture standing in wait for me, a grown-in-over-the-lawn branch of a dogwood tree. This branch made waxen white blossoms in the spring and ruddy foliage in the fall and, in between, made passes at me as I would stoop-plunge under it behind the power mower. If I was wearing a hat it would brush it off. If given a chance it would scratch my bald head. It would try to stick me in the eye. It would try to deposit, down the back of my neck, things that crawl. Every time I made the plunge through it I would close my eyes, for fear of losing one. Today the moment for which I had been waiting all these years finally arrived. I was out on the lawn early in the afternoon, with plenty of retirement time and nothing dictatorially urgent to do. I sat, for a time, and looked at the dogwood branch, and gave it a mock trial during which I recited, once again, its spring and fall contributions to the beauty of the yard, and invited in, for one last rebuttal, that combination of inertia and other more pressing things to do which had helped spare the branch in the past. Then I walked deliberately to the garage, took down the Swedish buck, sawed the errant bully of a limb right off at the trunk, pitched it onto the brush pile and, a few minutes later, walked very tall and straight through that edge of the lawn, the mower ahead of me and twenty years of petty servitude behind me at last.

Rules for a
One-Car Family

Tuesday, Oct. 10. The retirement conversion from a two- to a one-car family requires adjustments.

1. Never assume the car is going to be free for your own use. Always make any *thinking* you may do about using the car for any particular purpose at any particular time a *talking out loud* process, so that your co-user can hear and, if she has counter-necessities, announce them. (This morning, for the first, and, I hope, the last time, we discovered that each of us had been planning to take the car, at the same hour, in totally different directions. We solved the problem by getting C a pickup from one of her friends, but we both agreed we can't make that a regular imposition.)

2. Buy the gas yourself. (When there

were two cars, one his and one hers, with hers, the one used for family occasions or together-driving, she would occasionally buy gas, and even, on occasion, oil. But when there is only one car and she is certain he will be driving it in the immediate future, she will run out of gas before she buys any. It's your job to make sure she never does.)

3. Consider yourself fortunate if you married someone whose hip-to-gas-pedal measurement is close to your own. Otherwise, from now on, every time you enter the car, you have to go through contortions in order to twist yourself in behind the wheel and attain the position from which you can work the adjustment lever to get the seat back where it belongs.

4. Both should drive this car as if it were his and her last. Judging by the continuing trend in car prices, it may be.

Siesta, or Old
Man's Afternoon?

Wednesday, Oct. 11. One of the lightside editorial crusades I played with over the years was an attempt to introduce the blessings of the siesta to American life. In recent years I had begun to practice what I preached. I came home for lunch and, shortly after 12:30, couched myself for the first siesta of the day. I coached myself to wake up promptly at 1:15 and, presumably refreshed, go back to the short afternoon stint at the office. I would be home again at 3:30, when the routine schedule called for a second siesta, from which I recovered, supposedly in the mood for zestful outdoor activity, either in the garden or at tennis, at about 4:15. During these years I favored the siesta above any other part of the day. I was

74

proud of my disciplined ability to time it prudently. Extended beyond twenty minutes of actual sleep, the siesta can become a numbing, dulling experience. Within the proper time limit, it is precisely what an aging metabolism needs. The body relaxes and un-tenses itself. The mind, a playful, sometimes unbelievably inspired rover, flits back and forth between different worlds, sometimes weaving the two indistinguishably together. But retirement has brought problems. There is no need to wake up from the first siesta promptly because there is no office to go to. There is no excuse for the second siesta because there is no office to come home from. Minute by minute the habit seems to be resolving itself into one extended siesta. The longer a siesta lasts, the less magical its properties. It could deteriorate and prolong itself into an old man's afternoon. Even for daily siestas, as for weekends or for annual vacations, it is the counterbalancing work routine which provides the salt and savor.

Not Having to Twist
Nixon Around Any More

Thursday, Oct. 12. There must come to every pensioner the day when he realizes, with special delight, that he has probably been excused forever from an assignment he hated to have to do when he was earning, instead of just taking, a living. The shabbiest thing I had to do, when I had a job, was to pretend I had found convincing, worthy reasons for people to vote for their candidates for President. But this year I don't have to twist Richard Nixon around any more until he comes out as a candidate I can recommend to my readers. There is a certain irony in the fact that I come into this freedom in this McGovern year, when fabricating a logical and emotional case for Nixon might be even easier than it was against

Humphrey. But I'll take the freedom of not having to try, for Nixon or anybody else. I can, if I want to, go out and vote for a candidate for President without formulating any impressive list of reasons for my decision. I may lose or trample on my own soul, but I don't have to sell it, publicly, for mere wages. My only argument will be with myself. As for the past unpleasantness, that hasn't been just with Nixon. It was with Dewey before him, and with Johnson, and it might have been with Kennedy if he had lived to run again, and the only one it was never with was Eisenhower, who will, some day, be recognized as having been healthy for America. It was a good and proud thing to be for Ike, and he never let himself, or the editorial me-we, down except once — when he switched, in mid-morning, from his own instinctive candid honesty with Khrushchev on the U-2 incident to Cold-War-as-usual bravado. Later, out of office, and slipping into his dotage, he began to forget exactly what he *had* stood for, as old men, apparently, sometimes find it more comfortable to do. Come to think of it, Ike made one other mistake: keeping Nixon in 1952.

The Compulsive Gambler

Friday, Oct. 13. The real compulsion in the compulsive gambler is not to win, even though that flitting experience lights up the countenance and seems to raise the spirits. In reality a win, a big stroke of luck, merely raises the stakes and increases the odds the gambler has to overcome in order to reach his subconscious but ruling objective. That is to ·lose. The compulsive gambler is basically a masochistic creature, with gambling merely the most titillating device he can find for inflicting the most delicious kind of punishment on himself. At the track today, two things happened. First, going back to the track on the assumption that C's winning a daily double last month had opened a new way of life for us, we found out, the hard way, that the horses are not going to support our retirement budget. Second, I discovered that although I was outwardly bitter and disconsolate over my failure to make a single horse come in, there was, deeper inside me, a most illicit and dangerous peace and balm, as if I had somehow, in all this wholesale losing, found my own soul at last. It feels good to lose. Some people feed on being born losers. I may have admitted this to myself for the first time today, but I must have been tuning in on it all along, for why else would one choose to go to the track on Friday the thirteenth?

Moderation Happens
Like a Dream

Saturday, Oct. 14. To grow up in New England is to regard all life as a continual moral battleground, with all the sins and all the virtues wearing capital letters, as in *Pilgrim's Progress.* When a New Englander speaks of Idleness, he is referring to something he recognizes as the invention and instrument of the Devil. When he thinks of Moderation, his goal is a virtue worthy of all the fine resolves and mental and spiritual disciplines set down by Saint Emerson. All through life he finds it is indeed the idle moment which leads him to his indulgences and weaknesses, to drink, if that is his problem, to the cigarette, or to the nervous consumption of food, the greatest and probably the most harmful of all tranquilizers. Recognizing, and succumbing to, the temptations of Idleness, the New Englander wishes he could somehow amass the strength of will to save himself by the practice of Moderation. Then, one day, after a lifetime of such struggle, he finds himself merging into a state of retirement and realizes, with some dismay, that from now on his regular pattern of life is going to include an increasing number of moments in which he has nothing in particular to do except, if he yields to his own surviving indulgence, that of food, increase the number of snacks he has between breakfast and midnight. That was where this retiring New Englander found himself six short weeks ago. But somehow a miracle has occurred. Idleness is not necessarily an interval between snacks. In spite of greatly increased opportunities for calories, the weight is actually down from 178 to 168. The odd thing is that I have hardly noticed the decline, rather than the increase, in Gluttony which has been involved. There is, in all successful Moderation, something which is more of an effortless, quiet, dreamlike happening than the stirring result of any fierce making of resolutions or strong promises to one's self. You drift into a mode of behavior, and even seem to become a different assortment of chromosomes, and this happens without any great battle having been fought, and you do not preen yourself or compliment yourself on any great personal victory because it must, after all, have been a Mercy from On High.

Windy Sunday

Sunday, Oct. 15. The wind began before breakfast. It blew out of the north and it blew through the house, awakening the thermostat from its long summer holiday. It lashed the trees in the yard and it tormented the foliage landscape, so that all day long the leaves of many colors, near what the New England state development commissions label their peak display, had to fight to hold to their branch and not give up, this day at least, their summer lease on life. Fewer leaves actually fell, on this day of an incessant thirty- to forty-mile-an-hour wind straight from the north, than can be seen leaving the trees, almost any day at this time of year, under the impulse of much softer winds coming from the east or south. The direction of the twist may be important. Or it may be that the leaf, like people, surrenders to the softer touch. But today's wind, to give it credit, never paused to look behind and see what might be following it. All day it drove on past, sweeping the blue October sky clean of cloud and dust, beating the reds and yellows of the swamps and hillsides into a frenzy of resistance, striking through compromise clothing into old man's marrow, signaling, at last, the change of seasons which comes not by calendar but by how we live. Fifteen minutes before sunset the wind stopped, and the advance degrees of a whole winter of cold slipped in beneath the earth heat that, without hindrance from any clouds, was radiating swiftly, silently, up into the sky. Later the stars had their contradictory winter look, brighter yet more distant.

Being Your Own Handyman

Monday, Oct. 16. One in every five pensioners is a jack-of-all-trades who can do everything around his house and place and do it well. The other four are incompetents who, for their own safety, and for overpowering reasons both practical and aesthetic, ought to be forbidden any attempt to practice carpentry, masonry, or plumbing. Unfortunately their inability to afford to hire professional craftsmen for every incidental patch and repair job that comes along, plus the feeling that if jack-of-all-trades can do it, they also should be able to, impels them to make their own effort. The result brings great ugliness and mess into the world at ridiculous risk to their own physical safety. Work without knowhow is full of blunders, false steps, wrong-twist moves, hidden dangers. What it accomplishes is likely to be undependable in quality and grotesque to look at. What the forced-to-be-his-own-handyman leaves strewn behind him is a miniature demonstration of the kind of world it would be if it called upon its Adlai Stevensons to engineer its Brooklyn Bridges, its John Waynes to build its cities, and the genius of Rube Goldberg to hook things together. This dubious product is achieved only at great physical danger to the pensioner. Every move an old body makes in pursuit of some can-do it fancied it possessed in its youth is a risk. An unfortunate twist of a back muscle turns a twenty-dollar chore into a twenty-thousand-dollar medical expense. Today, patching the cement water run-off space alongside the cellar door, I was successful in those precautions advisable for my body age and my technical ignorance. So I would have lesser weights to handle, I bought the cement in eight forty-pound bags rather than in four eighty-pound bags. I mixed it in small batches. Not once did I find myself locked into the wrong kind of action twist. I escaped without physical injury. The cement job, however, looked as if it had been dribbled there by a cow. Whether it will last through the first cracking frost, or the first seeping rain, is a gamble. The one thing sure is that be-your-own-handyman has left his trademark, and is still on the loose, likely to strike again.

The Flesh One Loves

Tuesday, Oct. 17. I have been thinking about those ten pounds I have lost. They were, supposedly, a threat to health and safety; otherwise why the rejoicing over their disappearance? Yet there is also an instinct to mourn them with a certain tender affection. Those ten pounds, before inhuman abstinence shrank them out of existence, were *me,* the one and only precious me. They couldn't have grown on anybody else. They were the result of my own pleasant self-indulgence, a very personal permissiveness in which I let myself do the thing I wanted to do. And if I should spoil me, now and then, who has a better right? Or, to put the real question, who else would? I understand now, as I salute those lost ten pounds, how fat people feel about weight, how they can wrap that generous, warm fold of flesh around themselves and snuggle into a self-created cozy contentment which is impervious to the snide criticisms or imperative pressures of those who go around making a business out of urging fat people to reduce. This is their own fat, more precious than butter; the more they have to defend it, the more they love it. I am not really a fat person, myself. I am a thin person. But when I experience this special feeling about those ten pounds, I understand that sly, slightly incestuous feeling we all, in whatever class, have for our own flesh.

Don't Do Anything
Unless You Really Want To

Wednesday, Oct. 18. One big promise people ought to make to themselves as they enter the retirement phase is that they will not begin any new form of activity, pursue any new source of income, or undertake to deliver any kind of service or performance for anybody unless they are really eager to do the specific, particular thing involved. Nothing else, at this stage of life, can make any sense, no matter how convenient or fortuitous some new opportunity may seem to be. Unless, in terms of positive personal satisfaction, it is really worth some of the precious limited time which is all the time there is going to be for all that is left in life, it should be ignored. This was something I thought I knew until that moment when I allowed the discovery that somebody still wanted this old man, for pay, to overpower me. Yesterday I formally locked myself into the new commitment which puts me on the local town radio three times a week with a reading of the state political column I syndicate to five newspapers. The first performance went well enough. But today reality — that club which sneaks up on you and doesn't begin hitting you until you have already lost your chance for escape — began its attack. The truth was that I had, with the limited time and energy now at my disposal, settled for something I wasn't at all sure I really wanted to give any time, any energy, to. By such a commitment I had begun to close my new life down and in before it had really had a chance to open up. The warning to all who come after: Don't panic. Don't do anything unless you really want to.

Don't Be an
Optimist, Either

Thursday, Oct. 19. How swiftly fortunes turn, especially when they may be turning for the last time! Yesterday I regretted my own failure to reserve the rest of this little life for things that might prove to be big. Today there came a blow threatening to take away the one special thing which has been really big for me and which I had hoped might provide even greater satisfaction in this new and final chapter. This week's *New Yorker* had, in the lead "Notes and Comment" place I have been lucky enough to occupy at times (after E. B. White's retirement opened the door), someone else writing the same kind of piece Editor Shawn has been letting me supply. The publication of someone else's observations about a caterpillar was a particularly bitter blow because Shawn did have, in his office, pieces from me, in the light nature vein, which I would normally have hoped would be acceptable. If Shawn is reaching a crossroads in his kind, long-range relationship with me, the real reason may be something which pains his notoriously soft heart even while it devastates me — the possibility that now, at the very moment in my life when I should have time and concentration to write better than ever for *The New Yorker,* I have somehow lost whatever small sector of talent I once may have had, and will now be condemned to pressing too hard, trying to squeeze something fresh and natural out of perceptions and style which have gone dry. The biggest, most important part of my ego pleasure in life — and it may, if I can be kind to myself for a moment, be in part something better than that, like a capacity to give a touch of pleasure and recognition to others — is very near being gone. Did I say, at this point yesterday, don't panic? Don't be an optimist, either. As if to underline this point, a telephone call today made it final that the knave who took an option on these acres last spring, thereby putting rosy rainbows and pots of gold into my retirement anticipations, has decided not to renew his option. Twenty-four hours later I'm lucky to have that commonplace new job on the radio.

By Caterpillar
and by Pond

Friday, Oct. 20. I, too, not merely that new author of nature pieces for *The New Yorker,* have been looking at caterpillars this fall. Where he ostentatiously used the Latin name for them, and made money by pretending to be curious about why they would curl up in one leaf rather than another, I was concerned, as would be any proper dealer in nature lore, with the kind of winter they were predicting. That was easy; the caterpillars this year begin and end with heavy reaches of black fur and only a middle suspicion of January-thaw brown, which means a very early and a very hard winter, which has already been sampled by us in an unbelievable October snow storm the other day. What the caterpillars say is reinforced by the state of the pond, which is overflowing as it has not been this early in any previous year since we have been on the place. The adage, quite reliable through these thirty years I have been watching pond and winter together, is that winter fills its ponds before it freezes them. A long, hard winter? This is why so many retired people go south, to escape car trouble, shovel trouble, and heating bills. But not everybody wants to go south. I might not go south even if I had all kinds of checks from magazines and land developers.

Chauvinist Males

Saturday, Oct. 21. Whether or not women ever experience any particular tonic in situations of pure female companionship is something for mere males to speculate upon. Was there, in the separation of the sexes after the Victorian-style dinner party, any counterpart to the atmosphere of the cigars and strong talk? Is there, in the customs of the herds which include seasonal segregation, any female élan to match the lordly apartheid of the bucks and stags? One hopes so, for that would be only fair. Examine, for a moment, the atmosphere inside a car full of men on their way to some sporting event — the only situation which, in these days, is ever likely to create an opportunity for pure male companionship. Mark the ease of mutual acceptance and communication, the ready and cheerful chuckles of fraternal understanding, the uninhibited divulgence of privacies no one need fear will be used elsewhere or in any other context, the robustness of the assumption that each individual male in the company is lord and master of his own private domain back in the other world, the easy and natural wearing of the responsibility for decision, the reassuring backlog of past problems solved by such male decision-fortitude, the manly brace against occasional failures, honestly admitted, the recurrent talent for finding and saying the right words over all the facets of human experience, the frequent hand on neighboring knee, for attention or emphasis, the shaking together in convulsive laughter at some glorious quip that surprises even the mouth it happens to use, the gathering on the parapets of Beau Geste, the night-walking with Harry at Harfleur or Agincourt. All of which is a way of saying, to this journal, that we men went to the track today, and that there is no therapy for drooping spirits more instantly healing than an automobile full of innocently chauvinist males loosed, for the day, into the illusion they are free and bold and somehow superior. Going and coming it was good, and the losing horses in between meant nothing.

Who Runs the Thermostat?

Sunday, Oct. 22. Being at home regularly should bring to an end at last the war of the thermostat. There need be no more of the business of coming in from the office to find the house expensively overheated, no more of the domestic unpleasantness which then accompanies the remedial downward twist, no more discussion, from one evening to another, of just where the heating experts say the setting should be. The retirement life should mean, after the first meaningful assertion of watchful authority, the achievement of domestic peace and tranquility on the home heating front. The ideal system of control, now that circumstances make it possible, is obviously to agree on a standard, which I have done, and then stick to it, which is what I intend to do. There must be no more dual control tampering. One setting, from getting up until going to bed, should be enough. Occasionally, as I discovered today in one of my first days of operating the thermostat, there are conditions which dictate some variance. This was one of those fall days when the weather itself was on the borderline, indecisive about whether it wanted to call on the oil burner or not. A chill would come into the house and trigger the thermostat; the burner would ignite and send a pulse or two of warmth up through the first-in-line radiators; the thermostat would kick off and the burner go silent before any real impression had been made on the chill still in evidence through a great portion of the house. In such a situation, finding even the position at this desk unnecessarily uncomfortable, I employed my now uncontested authority over the thermostat decisively and usefully, and pushed the pointer up to seventy-two degrees until the house was fit to live in and work in. There didn't have to be any fuss or quarrel about it, as there so often was when I couldn't be home myself to keep a constant eye on things.

Building Your Own Dog House

Monday, Oct. 23. Building your own dog house doesn't necessarily have to end up with another "be your own handyman" mess. Whatever the architectural distinction of the result, the dog at least is certain to like it. And the actual process of putting together four sides and a roof, against all the minute technical difficulties lying in wait for the amateur, can have a therapeutic result, in which the successful contractor flatters himself that he is good for something after all. But these are after-the-deed conclusions. This morning it wasn't easy to decide to try design and carpentry for a dog house after all these years of vacation from building or making anything. It was difficult to find, around the place, either the right materials or the right tools. But a new dog is a necessity, and it has to be got now if it is to be big enough, next spring, to guard the garden against woodchucks. Today's time card on the project would have to read this way: Agonizing over having to do the job and looking for materials — 3 hrs.; trying to study out a design from available materials — 1 hr.; desperate phone calls to lumberyards finding out that unassembled dog houses cost $55 — 20 min.; renewed study of materials and possible design — 30 min.; sawing old lumber into design dimensions — 3 hrs. Result: pieces of prospective dog house almost ready for assembly, and the feeling, not .experienced in a very long time, not since, in fact, I first did anything handy as a boy, that perhaps, this day, I have been earning my keep.

We Can Make Laws and Will

Tuesday, Oct. 24. This is the birthday of the lost cause which must not be lost, the calendar anniversary of the murdered dream which will not die, the day on which, year after year, I have written in behalf of one special limited demonstration of what I believe to be the improvability of man. The United Nations is the symbol, forlorn now, but not forever, of the possibility that man may eventually become intelligent enough and political enough to make and enforce his law against the stupidity of war. I saw and hailed its birth, hoping, against hope, that the breeching blemish which included legality for regional alliances would not prove important. I watched it flower almost to its full potential in Korea, and so rejoiced in what seemed the main fact

— that an international police action had been taken, and successfully — that I managed to overlook the Truman-Acheson motives and the MacArthur perversion of what he might have made the most glorious command mission in all history. Again, without too close analysis of motive, I saluted Acheson's "united for peace" strengthening of the crisis authority of the General Assembly. And when, in 1956, Canada's great Pearson did the interior work while Eisenhower proclaimed that the law against aggression had to be enforced against our friends as well as against others, it seemed to me that the United Nations had, by two great improvisations, come close to the point where it ought to be ready to set itself up with full power to make and enforce law-and-order decisions. Then, before it had really mandated such power to itself, its own Secretariat carried its action beyond its writ by fighting in a civil war in the Congo. Meanwhile, Eisenhower left the Presidency to successors, each of whom — Kennedy, Johnson and Nixon —

contributed to a progressive downgrading of the United Nations in favor of the image of himself, as a single champion, defending his own version of law and order in the world. Today a hot war in Vietnam which is seven years old mocks the very existence of the United Nations, and it is the United States, a UN founder nation, which has consistently refused to recognize its jurisdiction. Nonetheless, I reaffirm all those years of editorial crusading in behalf of world law. It has been at least one proposition on which I have been totally and absolutely right; it will come because it has to come. To settle for any less a prospect, to slide off into the cynical sophisticated excuse that human nature will have to change first, would be to deny the possibility that human beings have intelligence. We can make laws, and will.

The Matinee

Wednesday, Oct. 25. Some things the male pensioner has to be broken to, like the theater matinee. The theater becomes logical for him because he now has more time and more need for such diversion. The matinee makes special sense because seats are cheaper and because, looking forward to winter, driving should be easier and safer. All this logic, unbeatable as it may seem, fades into disrepute soon after the pensioner, early on the scene as his pace of living now permits, settles into his sixth-row seat in the acoustical center of the center section. Today the first thing I noticed was the small number of men in the audience, only 12 out of the 250 seats filled. They were all very old and very feeble. That, at least, was a thought I had just before I lost consciousness. What I lost consciousness to was the rising tumult from women's voices. It filled the theater, on a surprisingly unmusical scale. Random phrases, suddenly floating up over the din, were instantly smothered back into the unintelligible insistence of more than two hundred throats all saying something at the same time into the same closed acoustic. It seemed to be that I had never before experienced such a claustrophobic dimension in sound, and that the limitless, crescendo volume of it would drive me out of my head. How could so many presumably soft voices build into such an unpleasantness? I complained to C, sitting quietly beside me, and she listened for a moment and then agreed. "The only way to escape from it," she said, with what seemed to be a hopeful suggestiveness, "is to begin talking to someone yourself."

Old Man's Puppy

Thursday, Oct. 26. After some noonday carpentry, which gave a rough finish to the dog house, and an afternoon of search which ranged from the Connecticut Humane Society's kennels to a final pet shop in Hartford, we came home with a puppy — a dark-faced, relatively unmarked shepherd-collie. She is, we hope, essentially the same dog we have always had on the place. Within five seconds of being put down on her new home ground, she had the heart of whichever one of us she ran to with tail wagging in a beginning of all the games she and we were going to play together. Still, this was not the usual kind of puppy homecoming. Hitherto, much of the tenderness of bringing a new puppy home was rooted in the fact that the puppy was being brought home to a child. The child and the puppy would grow up together, in mutual happy innocence, until they came to that tragic parting of the ways resulting from the difference in their life spans. The death of the dog who had once been their puppy — that was often, for the children, their first introduction to the ineffably sweet sadness of death, an emotional experience which at once awed and absorbed them by its compulsive, convulsive powers. This time, although SJ is home for vacation and was reenacting her own previous bringing home of her first puppy, this was not another child's puppy. It was an old man's puppy which came home today. The games she gets to play will be old man's games. He is to be her chief companion, and she will have to listen as he whispers to her some of his old man's problems. There is a different strain of sentiment in this kind of relationship, because now the life span of the puppy and the life span of the human being paired with the puppy have just about an equal number of years to run, if both are lucky. She is a lovely, gentle little lady, and we hope to find her a happy kind of name, one fit for a companionship to the end of a journey.

Euphoria, Via Yo-Yo

Friday, Oct. 27. There is no better therapy than that of building a dog house, and no better healer of the spirit than a puppy. Between the two, those doldrums — that spell of depression in which, feeling myself lashed by the world and its circumstance into a series of petty defeats, I also began lashing myself — have disappeared. The human spirit can stand only so much of one kind of feeling and then turns and twists, by whatever process it may take, by whatever degree of irrationality may be required, to something different. The dog house stands there, in front of the garage, a momentarily successful enterprise created by saw and hammer and nails. The puppy, still uneasy about unknown worlds, still flatteringly in love with the person it knows best in place of its mother, plays safely in the yard, away from the damage it might do gardens, away from the lifelong danger waiting for it out in the street. If a recovery of the spirit is inevitable and is going to happen anyway, these are at least substantive ingredients for the change. But the truth is that if it hadn't been a dog house and a puppy it would have been something else which produced this turn from depression to euphoria. Strip it down to its essential movements, and the human mood is as complicated as a yo-yo.

Farewell to Gin Forever?

Saturday, Oct. 28. I have trouble with the easy philosophy of Ecclesiastes that there is a time for everything. A time for farewell, when it means never, any more, tears the heart out of me. I am a sentimentalist half in love even with my own misfortunes and hardships. I never want anything to end — to change, perhaps, but not to end. So the realization that the regular Saturday noon game of gin rummy apparently went out of existence when I left my job and the office in which the game was played is sad and painful. This is not a reasonable or rational thing to say, but to measure by the sharpness of the pang I feel, the gin rummy is the one thing I am going to miss more than anything else — more than the opportunity to use the tools of the writing trade, more than the pay checks, more than the feeling of being part of a community function. Gin rummy is a deep game that unveils new subtleties, layer by layer, as long as one keeps playing it. I would guess that, over the years, it has given back a little more cash than it has taken. But the great kindness in the game is the way it always produces, on command, a head-to-head clash of skills and luck so vital, while it lasts, that it seems as if it were for life itself, and yet, the moment the encounter is over, the game becomes again a civilized pastime ready to be tucked away into its casual place. JM, the nucleus of the Saturday noon encounter, which sometimes expanded into a weird and riotous extravaganza with six people playing three games linked into one partnership score, has suggested that he might drop out to the house of a Saturday noon. This noon, as on the other two Saturdays which have elapsed since he mentioned the possibility, I found myself half waiting for him.

My Time Is My Time?

Sunday, Oct. 29. This morning, feeling as if I had overslept because the sun was already up and shining before I was, I hurried nervously from room to room and from clock to clock, setting them back an hour. Daylight saving is over, until the last Sunday in April. I have always resented the lack of imagination which keeps us going through this routine of switching afternoons to darkness at the very time of year they are growing much too short anyway. This afternoon, with cloud cover overhead, it had become full night at 5:30. It was a needless accentuation of the farewell to summer, a needless encroachment on the more useful end of the day. Most of all, it was a silly compliance with a mass inertia sensible people didn't have energy and influence enough to change. But suddenly, in the midst of my sullenness over this dark and dank afternoon, I realized that the system no longer really has any compulsion over me. I do not have to be anywhere Monday morning at any certain time. I do not have to be on Standard Time, or Daylight Saving Time, or any other kind of time except my own time. I am certainly in charge of my own rising. I can begin my day at whatever hour I please. I do not have to spend in bed that extra hour of daylight which has now been transferred to the morning half of the day.

I can get up in the dark and, so far as my own living is concerned, have as long an afternoon as the sun would be giving me if it were still Daylight Time. Does anything prevent any pensioner from going back to the original timepiece, the sun? I must study it out.

The Last of Leaves

Monday, Oct. 30. The dark gloom of that first Standard Time afternoon included a wild, twisting wind from the southeast of the kind (never, P.B.S., really from the west) that strips the tired and tattered autumn foliage down. This morning the yard and the landscape behind it had lost their colors; an October which had persisted all month in looking like a late September had become, overnight, a part of November. It is not very often that such a total change happens to a landscape overnight. Then, in the midst of desolation, in the place of the bright leaves, the scarlets and yellows of the maples, the rusts and bronzes of the oaks, something else began to move. There was, engaged in concentrated operation about the high-bush cranberry and its fruits, a flock of cedar waxwings, more easily identified now, in their small group gyrations, than when they had leaves to hide among. At another border, the wild multiflora rose hips had attracted a convention of robins, whose color, suddenly, became as vivid and as important as in early spring. The sadness of a world without leaves is deep and primeval, and not to be teased out of itself by the quick appearance of other and more animate colors flying. Nor is there, for those of pensioner age, any longer any quick and certain prophecy, in the last swirl of leaves, of the first greening of a new spring. But let it be put this way: It is pretty hard to catch New England nature without resource of some kind.

Afraid of Halloween

Tuesday, Oct. 31. The fear of the unknown is most powerful among the very young and the very old. With the very young the great curative, curiosity, usually comes to the rescue. With old people there is almost no curiosity as to which particular young neighborhood identity may be hiding beneath the Halloween mask at the door. With old people there is a dread, in this era of violence, of the possible appearance of tricksters a little older and meaner than children. With old people there are magnified memories, from past Halloweens, of such things as the soft vegetables splattered against the door, or the homemade bomb exploded in the mail box, or of the night long ago when adult friends, in playful mood, played their roles so well we didn't realize who they were until they had been hulking large and strange inside our home for too many strained minutes. But the real trouble with old people on Halloween is that there are no young people inside the house to go to the door, to play the guessing game with the tots, to muster the spirit to answer and mingle in the challenges of Halloween. So there comes the time when, instead of having jack-o'-lanterns burning in the window, the people in the house sit huddled into their deepest chairs, down below window-sill level, with as few lights as possible showing anywhere and no outside light at all, and try to let a television program distract their minds from the possible imminence of a knock on some door. Tonight the shameful, craven story was this: sitting in such fear, neither of us moved immediately when the one knock of the evening — a timid, two-thump-only knock — did come, and by the time one of us got to the door and turned on the outside light, what must have been a very small goblin had gone. We felt sorry for the small goblin, but more sorry for ourselves.

Clouds

Wednesday, Nov. 1. Spend an afternoon
with clouds. Have it temperate weather,
in which both sun and shade feel good on
the face. Make it several afternoons, one
each for the high etchings of the cirrus
and the low sheep-pasture chase of the
nimbus and one for those towering
cumulus battlements to heaven. As the
ceaseless parade of the clouds of any
particular day continues, it carries
uniqueness to the extravagant extremes
of which only the universal-infinite is
capable. No two formations are ever the
same. No single puff or castle remains the
same from one moment to another. And
no two human views of the same cloud in
the same instant can be exactly the same
unless they merge their separate angles

of vision into the common perspective of a camera lens. The cloud watcher invokes, by his mere willingness to watch, a command performance of a pageant which explores infinity. As infinity itself would free itself, should anyone try to imagine boundaries around boundlessness, the cloud watcher passes into a state of mindlessness. The clouds go over his body and his sight and through his consciousness and he also becomes a transparency, a thing of gossamer and happenchance condensation draped on a piece of lawn furniture. There should be more time, now, for the leisurely sensory approach to the majesties of our existence.

Is Social Security Manly?

Thursday, Nov. 2. Today the first checks arrived. Mine, by what detail of mysterious bureaucratic accounting I will never know, came out to be $253.60. The check for C came at $110. This is our Social Security nucleus of $363 a month for our future life. It is, of course, what I have been paying for and contributing to since January 1, 1937. Thanks to the special twenty per cent increase that went through Congress this summer, it is more than I had ever expected. Perhaps it is going to be enough, when put with everything else, to make it possible for us to continue to pay taxes on this land and heat this house. I remember back when Roosevelt was beginning Social Security, and I remember, very bitterly now that I am in receipt of this check, how some employers, in 1936, were putting slips into pay envelopes, warning that Social Security was going to be a scheme to defraud the workers. Now, today, this check in hand is a wonderful thing — a guarantee that one does not starve. Still, taking the check feels as if it were a two-way transaction of some sort — like that taking of the King's shilling, which bound the British subject to military service. If, as it feels, taking this check seals some kind of bargain, what is the bargain? Am I giving over, rendering, something more than those thirty-five years of payroll deductions? Am I a ward of the state? Am I something less of a success as a man, to be needing this kind of help? Does being on Social Security feel different from being on welfare, or living on charity, and, if so, by what degrees? The tentative answer has to be that, although I may find logic which says that my manhood has not been in any way diminished, the feeling that something left my life when these checks came into it will still persist.

The Three-Minute Egg

Friday, Nov. 3. Until this week, two months into our new way of life, it seemed that we were going to escape whatever emotional or personality jostling might result from putting two people into the same living space all day every day. True, there had been surprising instances in which C lost little time between a telephone call and her appearance ready for an unexpected shopping expedition with one of her friends. And there had been a few other occasions in which she seemed to be driving out of the yard just to get away from something. But there had been no serious symptoms of any kind until this week, when C began a strange campaign of improving on the three-minute egg. She claimed that something she read was responsible. You didn't really need to time, or even really boil, a boiled egg any more. Bring the water to a strong boil, pop the egg in, take the water off the burner, and then wait five minutes before serving the egg. This was supposed to produce an egg which was done just right, with velvet consistency. For us it produced an egg too runny and loose to eat. The next morning the egg that arrived on our plates was stiff and solid. "I went back to the four-minute system," C said. "Four minutes?" I inquired. "I thought we always had a three-minute egg." "I always cooked my three-minute egg for four minutes," C said. The third egg of the week, a three-minuter, came out right, but one could see that C was rebellious and unhappy over having cooked it only three minutes. The truth is, of course, that for forty years we have been cooking our three-minute eggs three minutes. Perhaps it is equally significant that, until this week, we never had boiled eggs three mornings in a row anyway. What may have come to the surface through this unexpected but very emphatic experimentation with the innocent morning egg is, I am forced to suspect, a very deep and perhaps desperate necessity on C's part to reach for some quick change in our pattern of living. Perhaps, subconsciously, she is trying to drive me out to Howard Johnson's for breakfast. Perhaps her whole life spirit is rebelling against the new life pattern it feels, not opening up, but closing in.

Deciding About Life
After Death

Saturday, Nov. 4. Today, with rain canceling outdoor projects and with all scheduled work at the desk caught up, I found myself sitting here with nothing to do but think. The likelihood of such opportunity — to think — is both the luxury and the dread of the pensioner state. Dread of such moments was, for sure, at the root of my lifelong desire to go out with job-boots on — to go in a moment of nothing but one blinding, overpowering realization while fingers were punching out some inconsequential last word. Today, in any case, here I was, sitting defenseless before my own thoughts, asking myself the kind of question I had always hoped to be too busy to ask. Do I believe in anything after this life? To pose such a question at this age is to realize that, if one is going to get an answer and have it ready, one is already close to the great big deadline — deathline, to be more specific. If I am ever going to know, for myself, what I believe, I have now reached the point of no postponement. So I try an answer, right here and now, thinking straight onto the typewriter. Do I believe something survives beyond the medical ritual of death? The first part of my present answer is crude and irreverent. I believe in playing all chances. But I do not wish to commit myself — am not able to commit myself except in the imagined extremity and fear and despair of some conscious death-bed scene — to a belief in the existence of any particular Guarantor (the fact that I capitalize this stand-in word is illustrative of the cute game I try to play) or any specific brand of survival (which is the workaday word for immortality and what we all really mean and seek). In my instinct to play all chances without making any normal kind of creed commitment I look for a low-priced, easy formula. Why not, by making the best I can of what I can do with myself and to others in the world as it is, keep myself prepared for all possibilities? Back in high school, the first poem anybody of my own age ever read to me with meaning was "Thanatopsis." It comes up now, quite as if it might have been, all this half-century in between, the most powerful and useful piece of sentiment saving itself inside me for rediscovery at some such moment as this. The convenient ethical strategy that suggests itself to me is this: Why not so live that when the summons comes to join that caravan, it makes no real difference whether there really is such a caravan or not? Life after death or no — how or why should that make any real difference in how one chooses to live this life? The convenience of this is that it seems to take care of everything except that embarrassing bit of genuflection to symbols and creeds I cannot quite accomplish and am not likely to be able to imitate unless it is in the dark terror of some frantically helpless and degrading (or saving?) last-moment scene.

Have We Been Around this Town Too Long?

Sunday, Nov. 5. We, who stay behind, and feel ourselves slightly chagrined by their easy willingness to shake what has hitherto been our common dust from their feet, are fond of predicting a tragic unhappiness for those people who, the moment they retire, yank up their roots and move to some new community which is completely strange to them. ''They are making a terrible mistake,'' we tell ourselves. ''How can they so nonchalantly give up a lifetime of friendship and association?'' we ask, and can puzzle out no answer. But they keep on moving out, to California, to Florida, to Arizona, to Georgia, and sometimes, without any rewarding change of climate at all, merely to another town in their own or a neighboring state. They never confess their error by moving back; they maintain an impregnable self-assurance in their correspondence or on their visits; even though they do not seem to have acquired new friendships or associations in any way comparable to those they had established in their local lifetimes, they do not admit to loneliness or hometown-sickness. Still, the perhaps wistful belief persists, among us who stay and who intend to stay, that there is something fundamentally wrong, and therefore necessarily unhappy, about spending a lifetime in one town and then moving elsewhere for a few last years during which the energy to communicate and the ability to get around will both be declining. Already, however, I can find within my own feelings one possible key.

By profession, for more than thirty years, I was constantly, functionally involved in the affairs of this town. This activity created routines and associations. But now this activity itself has been stopped, the functional friendships no longer have their particular reason for being, there are very few people I see regularly, and the affairs of this town, which I used to pretend to carry on one shoulder, no longer seem to concern or even interest me. As for the town, it wouldn't even notice if I left. Perhaps it is in some mood of mutually defiant ingratitude that the elderly, at the very end, renounce the scenes of their own lifetimes. But although I may agree that I owe the town nothing and it owes me nothing, and that the very idea of having roots here may be a fantasy, I do not intend to leave for something even less.

Are Senior Citizens
Good Citizens?

Monday, Nov. 6. Tomorrow, for the first time in this new condition of life, we are going to the polls, and, for the first time in all my life, I am really worried about how I am going to vote. I do not know, yet, how I am going to resolve the conflict between my sense of obligation to Nixon for having played the role in history — the journey to Peking, the apparent acceptance of peace without victory in Vietnam — which only he could have played, and, on the other hand, my emotional distaste for the man himself and my savage instinct to rebuke and punish him for the way he, even in his best policies and acts, insists on appealing to the worst, rather than the best, in people. But the voting chore that worries me most concerns a local bonding question authorizing $6,800,000 for enlarging the town's two junior high schools. For more than thirty years I, in my role of civic responsibility, have been urging others to vote yes on school spending questions. Tomorrow three things will be different. I have not, this time, committed myself by the way I have urged others to vote. We ourselves no longer have children in the school system. And tomorrow, for the first time, we will be senior citizens, our full earning power at an end. The biggest single drain on our reduced and fixed income is the property tax. Can I force myself, for the good of the community, for the sake of those other families whose children still have to be educated, to go out tomorrow and vote to take more tax dollars out of my own pocket? Shouldn't they take the vote away from senior citizens? I remember how I felt about them when we did have our children in school, and it was obvious that the older people were voting against any new school building no matter how badly it was needed. How do I feel about it myself, now that I may cast the same kind of vote?

Election Day With Ribicoff

Tuesday, Nov. 7. Abe Ribicoff was not running for anything today, and I, for the first time in forty-four years, was not involved in any election day newspaper chores. These personal circumstances, together with the obvious lack of drama in the voting going on — with McGovern, the candidate Ribicoff had nominated, heading for his terrible defeat — made it a curiously suitable day for the Senator and his new wife, Lois, to have us for luncheon at Tumblebrook Country Club. We have been through a lot of politics together since he first appeared in my office, making his first run for Congress in 1948 and using, as his introduction, the draft of a speech he proposed to deliver. The nature of that speech foreshadowed the whole building of his career. It deliberately posed a challenge to the national farm policy of his party — a show of independence which did not, however, run a very high risk of offending even the feed-buying farmers of his own Connecticut. In the ensuing years this handsome young fellow carried to its contemporary perfection the classic political art of not seeming to be the routine politician. He did his own thinking; he offered dramatic proofs of his talent for quarreling with political bosses; he parlayed these to a quick national reputation in the House at Washington, then back to two historic terms as Governor of Connecticut, then to the 1960 convention at Los Angeles and the Kennedy nomination, to the Kennedy Cabinet, and then, in circumstances no one has yet made clear to me, back to Connecticut to be a candidate for Senator. He comes up for his third term in 1974. There is no question the Senate, and nowhere else, is where he really wants to be. He wears both the open ease and the covert unease of the elder statesman; he knows what his own record should mean, in the way of political security; he cannot forget those unspeakable instances in politics when upstart challengers surprise the old champions. Today the conversation is philosophical and mellow and relaxed between friends who are taking this election day off and who take each other for granted. The interplay between the rising politician and the political columnist is almost over, now, and those instances in which one of us may have disappointed the other are fading in importance. All in all, he remains the best-balanced, most intelligent, most responsive political figure I have known.

Conscience Gets a Free Ride

Wednesday, Nov. 8. I cast my first votes as a senior citizen yesterday. First, operating on sheer willpower, I voted for the $6,800,000 school bond issue, thus escaping, for the moment, the instinct of the elderly taxpayer to be against all public spending. The second major decision waiting for me inside the voting machine confronted me with the name of Richard Nixon, and asked me whether I was going to keep an implicit bargain I once made with him, without, of course, his ever knowing it. When he first began moving troops out of Vietnam I pledged that, if he continued to do things in foreign policy only some famous anti-Communist Republican President could accomplish safely, he would have my support and gratitude no matter how much the personal chemistry of the man came to offend me. My arm felt a flood of reluctance as it reached toward his lever, but it reached, and pulled it down, and my part of the bargain, in spite of instincts which distrusted and disliked him as much as he ever disliked and distrusted the Communists, had been kept. The result of the voting today was that the school issue lost by a margin my vote could not prevent, and that Nixon won by a landslide that made my contribution to it inconsequential. I had, in effect, had a free ride for my conscience, being able to follow it without having it cost me. What a pleasant luxury, to be able to do the right thing and not suffer for it!

No Comment

Thursday, Nov. 9. For forty years, instant comment on great events was the kind of brick I made, the machine process I operated, the nut I turned on the chassis of life as it came past me on the assembly line. I developed a routine proficiency at it. I thought, lived, ate and slept my particular function. It was something that had to be done, or at least faked, every day. It always seemed that something would happen if I did not perform. And over the years there built up, as is perhaps necessary for any working man who has to survive his own occupation philosophically, the feeling that what I did was not only important in itself, but especially important because I had a knack for doing it especially well. But now today is the second day after the great Nixon re-election, and I have not made comment on it. I have had some ideas — like how much I hold it against McGovern that he and his followers may have damaged the liberal cause for years to come with their irresponsible carelessness of word and deed — but I have not carried them through, because there has been no functional need to do so. I would like to be doing a piece, too, on how, in this age of television images, the regional candidates who seemed to do best were those who went on neighborhood-to-neighborhood walking tours among their constituents. But there is no requirement I get these thoughts into shape to put on paper, and no place for them to be published if I should, and the great world outside this room is making do for itself, thank you, just as if I and my small proficiency had never existed. Does such vivid demonstration that you are not needed now mean that you never were? To hell with that thought. Besides, they weren't bricks. They were pearls.

I Have Been Very Careful Not To

Friday, Nov. 10. If a woman gets it into her head that a certain type of behavior is to be expected from one of us imperfect males, she is always going to find the moment when she proclaims that he has actually done it. Sooner or later C was certain to turn on me triumphantly and say: "See, this is what they all say is the very worst thing about having their husbands around all the time; they try to take over in the kitchen." Precisely because I have known that she has been waiting to say this, I have been especially careful not to create the slightest opportunity for her. Tonight, when she finally used it on me, it seemed to me that she was being deliberately reckless with her accusation. All I had done was to go out in the kitchen and, without saying a word, lift the cover from the pan in which the pork chops were smoldering, sniff, and put the cover back on, a truly dead-pan, noncommital performance in which there wasn't the slightest trace of comment or opinion, even though we both know that we both know that she has a habit of overcooking pork. It is true that I have had time to notice a few kitchen procedures about which, if it were permitted, I might make a suggestion, but I have been scrupulously self-disciplined about all of them. Now I have been accused anyway; the woman has proclaimed woman's prophecy fulfilled; perhaps, I might as well, some day, commit the crime of which I have been pronounced guilty. As for the pork chops, they were done just right, but perhaps only because C took them off the burner soon after I, in my innocent pursuit of an appetizing smell, had called attention to their advanced condition.

The Vacuuming I Abhor

Saturday, Nov. 11. It gets into a house by sticking its foot in the door. Once in, it is in constant need of repair. Somebody runs it through the house at various intervals. And that, for all the blessed years of a man's full-time employment, is all he knows and all he needs to know about the vacuum cleaner. This morning my long insulation from the grim side of the housekeeping operation came to an end. Just as I was trying to get settled peacefully at this typewriter C began dragging something up the open stairs to the room directly overhead, and was soon attacking that many-cornered bedchamber with an oppressive thoroughness which, no matter how high the ungodly, inhuman whine of the machine was pressed, never seemed satisfied. Occasionally, between upstairs rooms, the sound would cease, and C would come down the stairs past my door. But when I looked for a possible friendly word of apology for infringement on the quiet I need for significant accomplishment at this desk, I seemed to detect only a firm suffering look which might have been saying: "You think you are going to be around the house this way the rest of your life without hearing a vacuum? I'm sorry, but this is the way it is going to have to be when there is housework that has to be done. This, incidentally, is the way it has been all those years when you probably thought the house cleaned itself." If there was, in C's look, such a touch of cool reproof, I admit, in the chastened wisdom of this morning's experience, that I deserve it. I wouldn't wish running, or hearing, a vacuum cleaner on anybody. How can a supposed boon to the housewife, purportedly invented and designed to make things easier for her, do such a terribly savage job of tearing home and mind apart?

The Mirage of the Unselfish Act

Sunday, Nov. 12. What kind of people-animal are we? I am trying to remember, in one of those desperate auditing moods that begin to occur once one finally admits his age, a single instance in which some truly unselfish act — or even thought — may have been part of me. One has to rule out situations in which one's vanity may compel that action which seems most likely to be judged, by a watching world, to be heroic and self-sacrificing. The kind of test which really counts is the test in which there is no obvious warning that anybody is watching, and where the likelihood is that the only judgment to be encountered is merely one's own. In such a situation, would I choose — or have I ever chosen —

the act which puts someone else's welfare and happiness ahead of my own? Ironically, it is about time I began trying such an honest, if dismal, accounting of my own actions and motivations, because I myself have always lived in a rather silly romantic expectation that other people, for no very good reason except the goodness of their heart and their uncontrollable admiration for me, were about to give wonderful gifts or make dreamlike things happen for me. All my life I have been half expecting, from others, the kind of volunteer help which I myself have never given. I must still try to discover, in my memory, or, perhaps in some future moment of thought or choice or action, some instance in which I do not think of myself first and serve myself first and only. Perhaps I will be lucky. Perhaps there have been, or are still to be, on the record, some of those "little, nameless, unremembered acts Of kindness and of love" which Wordsworth claimed to know about. What a good warm inner feeling — so close to the final audit — that could be!

The Group Luncheon

Monday, Nov. 13. All that vacuuming was part of the preparation for today, when milady was, for the first time in our new life, entertaining one of her "groups" for luncheon. For years I have been picking up bits and pieces about the format and content of these gatherings. There is a topic for discussion, based on a book or play. Somehow, perhaps while they are permitting themselves a sip of sherry before they sit down to eat, they manage an exchange of the social intelligences of the week. The luncheon itself is invariably based on some dish the hostess can prepare in advance, so that she does not have to absent herself from the discussion in order to produce it. Afterwards, there is supposed to be a general request for the recipe. Shortly after three o'clock the ladies leave, to resume their respective domestic obligations. That is the pattern for the group luncheon day. Occasionally, a husband is sick and becomes an off-stage presence in the hostess house. And there are husbands who come home for their own lunch, in a separate room, and who then display their plumage, for a graceful moment or two, in front of the ladies. Today I had C pack me a lunch, which I ate in the press room at the State Capitol. I went to the state library and worked my way through two years of newspaper files; I went to the radio station and straightened out some tapes; I went to the supermarket and bought pet food. But finally I came to the point where I had neither idea nor energy for doing anything else that would keep me away from home. The girls were still here. I kissed the dear one whose birthday it was. They were all bright and happy and nice to me. It was a vivid scene to walk into and be welcomed into. Nevertheless, I had the feeling that my intrusion was bruising the membranes of a very special mystique I never would, and perhaps had better not, understand. There was something in the air, something quite apart from all the many things men fancy they can get from or share with women, which was not to be defined and possessed, not even in a thought.

Barkis

Tuesday, Nov. 14. The family has now finally realized with how subtle and talented a hand it has been ruled all these years. The "old man's puppy" arrived without a name. There has always been an assumption in the family that whoever named a pet was somehow closer to it, more its special owner, than anybody else. It wasn't until, waiting calmly for the rest of us to be uninspired, C had solved the problem of a name for this pet that we all realized that she had always been performing this vital service without ever claiming any special credit or reward for it. She named the last dog Chris because he came home on Columbus Day. She named the black cat Angela after Angela Davis. It had to be changed, on closer examination, to Angelo, as a matter of grammatical gender. Now she has named the puppy Barkis. She solves the question of gender by pretending that Peggotty, after marriage, continued in service and was henceforth addressed by her new surname. By selecting Barkis she somehow links, in her mind, and in mine too, I confess, the new puppy with far-off first days here on the farm, when this small office room was then the fireplace-heated family room for nightly readings from Dickens. After making the choice, and making it stick, even to the immediate response of the puppy herself, C has reinforced her nomenclature by serendipitous encounters with a dog named Barkus in the *The Thurber Carnival* and, in the *Odyssey,* a dog named Argus who recognized the returning Ulysses before Penelope did.

The old man's puppy has been named for him. Barkis is Barkis.

The Pleasure of Reading Rediscovered

Wednesday, Nov. 15. I now begin to rediscover, with almost as much of a thrill as when the first black marks on white paper turned themselves into a dog or cat that could always be found there whenever a very small boy wanted them, the magical privilege of reading for pleasure. A lifetime of reading for functional purposes, for assignment, for information, had given both eye and brain a certain professional competence and developed speed and efficiency at the expense of all that naïve wonder which ought to well up into all one's senses the moment that first of the senses focuses on the printed page. That printed page, if surrendered to, may soon make one see, hear, smell, taste and touch all that has ever existed, or may ever exist, within or beyond the experience and mind of man. I begin to associate again with the wonderful voices, the intimate discoveries, the intense emotions, the artful changes of pulse, the unexpected liberations of mind, the titillations of spirit, and, from all the senses, that sixth and most enviable, the sense of well-being, all packaged into the encounter with representational marks on paper. What greater wealth than the warm possession of a page of print, ready to take you into some world of your own special choosing, or, for that matter, into a world so strange you have never hitherto even imagined it! What a luxury to be able to curl up, in embryo position, while two minds, the one in the page, the one behind your own eyes, engage in uninhibited, seminal, puerperal play with one another! It is hard to believe that so wonderful a gift could be something man has made for himself, all by himself. There must have been tablets, handed out from burning bushes on mountain tops. That is the feeling I have been experiencing lately — as if I had just been handed one.

Between Meals

Thursday, Nov. 16. Eating between meals has to stop. Indulgence, in this loose-schedule last lap of this mortal journey, carries doubled Dantean dangers for both mind and body. I have sense enough to be afraid. And I have discovered, in short order, that it is no cure, no safety, to try to establish any time routines or calorie rules for snack-breaks of any kind. If there is to be an eleven o'clock nibble on some dry health cracker, it inevitably advances itself to a ten o'clock mouthful of rich cookie. Only one thing works. That is to train yourself to turn off the thought. One must, quite deliberately, exercise the same mental control one sometimes learns to use for an arthritic pain. If a knuckle begins to throb, it is sometimes possible, by a sheer act of will, to make the pain move somewhere else and then get lost. If I allow the between-meals temptation to stay up here in my mind and down there in my gut nervous system, while I undertake to fight it, the indulgence always wins. Let the idea keep nibbling away, and you lose. But dislodge it, and then go on, matter-of-factly, to some other immediate engagement for both mind and body, and you are a winner. Let me try a specific example: This is the 16th of November, and there are still Halloween Hershey bars out in the yellow bowl in the pantry. I have been very strong, leaving them alone. It is sixteen days they have been there. The last time I counted, there were still thirteen of them. No one would ever notice if one of them was gone. There is no one here in the house with me. Naturally, I wouldn't, or couldn't, make a regular thing of it. There would be no way, at least not until next

Halloween, to bring any more into the house. Eventually the almonds go stale. Hershey bars today are much smaller than they used to be. In any case, it's time to stretch the old legs for a few minutes.

Senior Citizens at Bay

Friday, Nov. 17. Every new pensioner must be familiar with the kind of phone call which came last night: "This is John Doe, calling about your contribution to the United Fund. I have your card here showing that last year you gave fifty dollars. Are you planning to match it this time, or can we hope for a little more?" Similar business comes to the front door. There are collections, with the canvassers usually your neighbors, for the various health funds. There are the Girl Scouts with their smiling faces and their cookies. There are young weirdos who ask you to believe they are working their way through graduate school. In the mails come, periodically, letters from the class fund, and the alumni fund, of the college you yourself worked your way through, forty-five years ago. Finally, there are testimonial dinners, with the price of the tickets high enough to finance a gift. Very often these dinners are for people you would very much like to honor and applaud. For all these situations, the senior citizen needs not only a philosophy, to satisfy himself, but also an answer, to give to the outside world's often innocent solicitation. Face up to one thing. There is no happy solution. To say no to everything is not only an embarrassment in itself, not always easily or graciously understood by the other parties involved; it also kills one more involvement with the energetic world of happenings and movements. To say yes, on a reduced scale where scale is possible, but yes, even if it means some tight pocketbooking in some other area, is the more pleasant course. Life — being and feeling part of life — is still the number one necessity. If, like most pensioners, you must economize, try to accomplish most of it inside your own private world, not by cutting lines to the outside. Personal interpretation: I will still, at the least, buy Girl Scout smiles.

On Borrowed Furniture

Saturday, Nov. 18. Thirty years ago, when we were moving into this big house without the beginning of furniture enough for all its rooms, our music teacher was breaking up her home and leaving town and had a number of pieces she wanted to store, with privileges of use, until she herself might have a place for them again. Over the ensuing years, there have been surprise occasions when Mrs. D. would appear and take back a piece or two, and other moments when she was threatening to do more. But last September, soon after I left work, Mrs. D.

wrote, quite without knowledge of our circumstance, of course, that she was now making her own final retirement move and would want her furniture back. This, for us, meant expensive replacements at the very stage in life we could least afford them. It was such a severe blow, in prospect, that C and I were not even able to talk very much about it. We kept it at arm's length as a problem too big for us to try to solve. Yet we knew we were both thinking about it, all the time. Still it was not with any idea at all of doing anything about our own furniture plight that we headed, this noon, for the annual Rotary Club antique show at the high school. Occasionally, when she has no one else to go with, I accompany C to a show, and sometimes we see a piece we think would be beautiful to own if we could afford it, and that is all an antique show has ever been. I have never had my checkbook out. But today, one third of the way down the first aisle, we found ourselves in a booth which was our reconstructed living room.

The Whole Booth

Sunday, Nov. 19. Late this Sunday afternoon, as the Rotary Club's antique show was closing down, our new furniture came home. In the booth we entered, almost as if with *déjà vu,* there had been four main pieces — a sofa, an Empire table, a pedestal table, and a coffee table of obvious homemade origin from an era that never made coffee tables as such, which was the first piece that really spoke to us. It offered itself not as a replacement for anything Mrs. D. owned, but as the ultimate special piece C had always been looking for to have in front of Mrs. D.'s sofa. The sofa in the booth, wearing a fabric that harmonized with the existing colors in our front room, spoke next. The Empire table looked to be the near duplicate, although more lustrous, of the one Mrs. D. was going to reclaim. As for the pedestal table, it had no relationship to anything Mrs. D. might be taking, but was a style of table C had always lingered over at every show we attended together. Standing in this seemingly fatefully assembled replacement living room, we tried to maintain our self-control. In fact, we succeeded in walking out, telling the young dealer we were going home to measure the space the sofa might occupy, and telling him we might possibly be back. Instead of going home we went to lunch, but in the midst of her sandwich C said she hoped no one else had noticed the coffee table. After her admission she liked the piece that much we hurried home, not so much to measure the sofa space, which we did, as to get my checkbook. Back at the high school we found the exhibit intact. The check was written, and I, the iron-willed holdout who had never before yielded to the temptations of the antique game, had plunged in and made my first operation — one in which I cleaned out an entire booth.

This afternoon the new room arrived. We have survived the crisis Mrs. D. was precipitating. We have a few things of our own. I may spend a day here, some day, just looking at the lovely soft piece which now stands where our old coffee table, modern and cheap and one thing Mrs. D. could not take because it was, sadly enough, our own, used to stand.

I Could Tell the World How Right I Was

Monday, Nov. 20. Today, for the first time, it hurt not to be working. Where it seemed a blessing not to have to concoct comment and opinion on the dismal Nixon-McGovern farce of a Presidential contest, it feels like an unjust punishment when I am not able to rip up and down these typewriter keys a few times in celebration of the fact that Willy Brandt, in the West German elections yesterday, finally succeeded in leading the Germans toward an exit from the insanity in which American policy, inspired by such as Acheson and aided by Adenauer, had so long imprisoned them. If there was one thing I think I was right about over the years, it was the total error of splitting Germany into allies for the respective sides of the Cold War, and the prophecy that if we didn't come to our senses the Germans themselves would one day take their own initiative out of such historic nonsense, perhaps in ways that would not please us. Willy Brandt ought to have our gratitude instead of our grudging tolerance (I refer to our official Washington attitude) because he has begun the process of healing and reuniting Germany and ending World War II in the gentlest and most reasonable fashion. Some measure of victory for what I have believed in and have been writing about for so long seems close, now that the German people themselves have made it clear they are beginning to understand and appreciate what Brandt is trying to do. I don't know whether the way I feel today means that I retain as great an interest as ever in the affairs which used to be clay for my bricks, which used to signal for the turn of the screw I made at my place in the assembly line. Perhaps this is merely a temporary nostalgia, triggered by unusually appealing news. I would feel better — or would I? — if some working commentator had it in him to produce the kind of piece I would be writing today, if I were working. False modesty to the winds, I was right, and almost alone among editorial writers, on a few things — not that it ever did, or does, matter in the slightest, except to me.

Paean to Politics

Tuesday, Nov. 21. When I think of politics I think of the people, the voters, as a vast sea, whose tides and currents and temperatures can never be charted and gauged with any final accuracy until one actually plunges into them. And I think of the candidate (and sometimes the party, when that seems animate) as the individual who is driven and encouraged, by his own varying motivations, to make the plunge that tests the will and disposition and mood and intelligence of the people-ocean. He must hold nothing back. He is not permitted to dive obliquely; he must plunge, his arms spread wide as in an appeal, so that he takes the potentially crushing impact full on his chest. Sometimes, if he is a natural and the elements are kind, the people-ocean receives him and bears him up as if he were the proud prow of a swan. Sometimes, if he is really out of his element and the odds against him are relentless, the awkward impact crushes the breath and hope out of him, so that he never manages a stroke, but is merely floated, inert, over into the backward eddies where might-have-beens turn into lily pads. The average plunger encounters neither instant success nor disaster, but wins, by his leap, a hard-working, career-long chance to match his strengths, his skills, his intuitions and his lucks against the perpetual mystery of the great body politic. Of those I have seen take the plunge, FDR did so most magnificently and triumphantly, the swan if there ever was one, while Richard Nixon has been the graceless ugly duckling, imprisoned in a long and unequal struggle. But for them all, even for those whose names would mean nothing because their plunge failed to survive itself, I feel a great love. I admire and envy those who take the great gamble, on themselves, on people.

Turning off a Few Lights

Wednesday, Nov. 22. Perhaps tonight was a little worse than usual, because it was the night before Thanksgiving, and C always likes to have the house full of lights as a sign of welcome during the holiday season. But there have been non-holiday nights, all fall, when our use of current has seemed excessive. I have been going around night after night checking on what lights are really being used and then surreptitiously turning off a bulb here and there. We don't talk very much about my new concern with the lights. Once, when C noticed that I was going around turning off a few, she made a guess, out loud, that our electric light bill was probably lower than that of anybody we knew, and the way she said this conveyed the impression that she thought that I, in some silly play-acting of my retirement role, was developing an excessive concern for petty economies. Strangely enough, my own impression was that it was only since we had been on this fixed-reduced-income basis that she had developed such a special passion for light. Anyway, there is getting to be a typical evening story in this house: Come the dusk, C goes around turning on a few lights. A little later, I begin going around seeing how many I can turn off. Except that tonight, I didn't operate at all. People are coming home for the holiday. It is good to have the lights up. We will have to get down to the realistic facts of life — about how the pennies have to be counted if we are to have dollars enough to get by on, and about whether the worry over pennies is worth it, anyway — at some later time.

Holiday Thoughts

Thursday, Nov. 23. Today's thoughts have been of a lifetime's succession of Thanksgivings. First came the sheer tingle and joy of childhood gatherings and feasts, when we were passionate for ritual and pleasure provided by somebody else. Next there was the sweet and satisfying time of life when we began providing Thanksgiving for ourselves and our own children. Finally there comes the observance which is more an obedience to tradition than a celebratory pleasure. For some time past, our Thanksgivings have seemed to belong in this last classification until, like Christmas, but never to such an intense degree, they have seemed holidays cursed with a feeling of artificiality, something to be endured rather than enjoyed. In place of the excitement of childhood and the warm satisfaction of the years of the growing family, the gift of the holiday becomes the perverse, jangling, psychological and physiological upset which afflicts jet travelers who are whisked brutally from one time zone to another. It takes weeks to recover from the shock of living through the claustrophobic pressurized-cabin imprisonment of a long holiday weekend; the trouble is that Christmas itself is now only a few weeks away. As always, when I indulge in such thoughts, I am ashamed of having had them. Sometimes I force myself to admit the truth, which was today, for instance, that there had never been a nicer Thanksgiving, with C serene and capable, the mid-afternoon dining slow and pleasant, the two children home in good form, the traditional guest the warm, good friend of always. Nice to have it. Nice to have it over.

Fun and Games

Friday, Nov. 24. In that young age when fun and pleasure were all in all and holidays were times of crowded rooms, the thing that would make a young heart really burst with happiness would be the miraculous development of a decision that a game would be played. Flinch, Lotto, Pit — the more people could fit around the dining-room table the merrier, the more breathlessly happy the evening, sad only when it always had to come to an end and yield its players back to the humdrum of the great non-holiday expanse of the year. Tonight it was still holiday. The thoughtful provider, K, had brought a game. At the sacrifice of programs no one really cared very much about seeing, we turned off the television and played the game. It was not the sheer, suspenseful fun of childhood. But even adult families should play something together a few times a year. If we didn't play together and thus gently force a little mutual pleasure, we would separate into cool, boring individual compartments for the rest of the evening, wondering, perhaps, what had become of family. We played with mild enthusiasms, occasionally happy spontaneities of friendly rivalry. But when, toward eleven o'clock, the second contest of the evening had been completed, no one had either voice or instinct to start another. It was good, as with the holiday itself, to have the play, but good to have it end. Always, in such an experience, we ask ourselves: Was this the way our elders felt about playing games, when we were young with our hearts bursting with eagerness to have everybody play everything forever? If they felt this way, what a debt we owe them, for all the hours when, tired and ready for rest, they sat up straight and sported with us in spirited fashion! Or were they, perhaps, more fortunate than we, or better human beings than we are, and gifted with the grace and love that enabled them, on every holiday occasion, to turn as young as their youngest — or, even in later years, when all were hopelessly adult, to cherish, without effort, the forms of former pleasures?

Do People Still Have Friendships?

Saturday, Nov. 25. I was visited today by the son of the man who was, for many years, the one I would have named, if pressed, as my best friend. Our situation had been that, when and if we had to turn to someone, it would be to each other first. Our families had holidays together. When he died, one chapter in my life closed, too. Yet, other than being able to sense that, if one needed the other, he would be there, without question, we exchanged no words of friendship. We were not even particularly good in each other's company. He never gambled, which was what I liked to do most with other men. I never went with him on fishing trips, which were what he liked to do with other men. Each of us may have wished that something more could be made of our relationship; our small town backgrounds gave us each memories of how our elders, in our childhood days, had apparently enjoyed deep and fast regular friendship rituals in which they found themselves often together without having to arrange it or make dates with one another. I think I remember that we did, on at least one occasion, bemoan the passing of the old drop-in ways of established friends, as if we were suggesting that, if we had lived back then, we would have been together a great deal more. That may have been our mutual confession that we had a friendship, but that it was not any Damon and Pythias idyll.

What occurred today had the curious effect of reviving that friendship and making it much more real than it ever seemed to be during our actual journey through it. His son dropped in and, as soon as he had the opportunity, said he had come to see me alone, about a personal matter. We went into a closed room, and it was a personal matter, and he was consulting me because I had been his father's best friend, the one he was choosing for understanding and counsel in what had become, for him, a choice of roads situation. I somehow managed to rise toward the occasion, and talk to him with at least a simulation of wisdom, but also with something else that was no simulation at all. I found I was speaking to him in a mood of great affection and love for him, and I know, in various ways, that he was touched. And I hope he has been helped; I hope some wisdom greater than my own, something rooted, perhaps, in love, did reach out and help him toward the decision which is best for his career. But what he had done for me, meanwhile, with his Victorian gesture, was to prove how much more deep and real than its own participants had ever realized the original friendship had been.

The Young Barkis

Sunday, Nov. 26. Here the old man is, on the far side of this vale of tears, this experience in the arts of relinquishment and resignation, this "long fool's errand" — here the old man is, once more engaged, perhaps for the very last time, in the business of chaperoning youth. The youth is Barkis, the old man's puppy. She has grown six inches longer and a couple of inches higher. Her coat has begun to fuzz out and provide better warmth for her nights out alone in the dog house. She likes, when she has been released from her rope, to be picked up and held for a few moments before she unleashes her first run at the cats or begins visiting the spots she has begun to know. Her heart beats wildly against the arm that holds her. After she has chased cats she comes back, looking for a shoe lace or a pants cuff or a hand she can pretend to bite and chew, while making fierce little growls. She begins to like to walk, and today, for the first time, she began to run ahead, turning and waiting, now and then, for me to catch up. Until today she had been following always, almost under my heels. Occasionally, scratched by a briar or nose made sneezy by some careless rush into some reality, she turns to me with an uncomprehending whimper. Otherwise she is still free of any real experience of restriction or denial or discipline. Sometimes people who, following their own life instincts, have participated in the bringing of new life into this world, come to a time when they feel like criminals for gestating so much innocence and then condemning it to so much woe. And here I am, doing it once more, as if I would never learn. This happy, innocent Barkis, this embodiment of pure joy, is taking my hand trustingly and affectionately, as if the world I will lead her to is all desire and fun and no disappointment and regret. I begin to feel the guilt; I wish I could make it up to her; I wish I could change the world for her.

Worship

Monday, Nov. 27. Now in the late afternoons the sun hesitates a few horizontal moments before it sinks below the western line of hills. As it shines back over the fields and settlements and city squares it gave light and some warmth to during the day, it has the kind of clear focusing on the landscape it never attains in foliage-filled summer evenings. Here, angling between clouds and hills, it illuminates and gives life and habitation to a group of houses one never notices at other times of the year. It finds, and turns golden, the straw-colored cones clustered in the top of a spruce. It catches all of itself in some distant single window, and flares back on itself as if it were baffled flame. It follows its surveyor lines across a valley to make a patch of summer seem to bloom again on a hillside far beyond halloa. Although it has, by this hour of this day in this season, lost all warmth, it projects, more brilliantly than ever, its light and color, its memory and its promise. Now, when the leaves are gone that bewildered and diffused, into dancing patterns of their own, the level evening rays of summer, now, in the time of the negative solstice, when earth and blood seem to slow down as if they might not start up again, the sun still is the sun the sun the sun the sun.

De Senectute in the Flesh

Tuesday, Nov. 28. Tonight, at Long Wharf Theater in New Haven, David Storey's *The Changing Room*. Although I could have availed myself of many opportunities during this decade of total license on stage and screen, this happens to be the first time I have seen total nudity. It is my luck that this first experience is with the male body — a whole room full of male bodies, and young male bodies at that. They are all smooth, hard bellies and, although there are variations in what hangs below the bellies, the composite impression is one of masculine equipment magnificent in structure and in potential. And I, an old man, sit there watching their youthful flesh and power cavort about the stage, and cannot help exulting in it as an affirmation of masculinity in the tribal sense even while I also experience the bitter chagrin, as an individual, of feeling hopelessly and irretrievably inferior to it. Some things one says goodbye to long before the journey ends. The fresh, pure, unbidden vigor of sex is one of them, and it may be the life force, it may be all there is. Perhaps that is the reason why, no matter how many times we think we say our goodbyes, it never does die, never does surrender. They don't stop making beautiful bodies. There is no winter season shut-off for thought and feeling. Seeing a stage full of prancing priapic virility is an affirmation of one's own membership in the sacred cult, the confraternity, of the procreative male. The inequality of it is primordial, and not to be exorcised by modern slogan or creed or Constitutional amendment.

Pre-Winter Afternoon

Wednesday, Nov. 29. There are dividends in having time free for the place, and these shortening afternoons, when the duration of the sun so closely matches my physical endurance, often make satisfying packages of activity. Today, by ending siesta at 1:30, I bought myself as much outdoor time as I felt like using. I took pictures for C of her Christmas cactus, which is budding in a profusion that excites us. Shooting from outside, through the plant-room window, I stepped into the spot where our homemade bird feeder traditionally stands. If the Christmas cactus is beginning to bloom, it is time to set the feeder up again. It consists of a section of old water pipe which is driven into the ground and an 18-inch-diameter slab of elm into which a long bolt has been fixed. The bolt fits into the top end of the pipe, and as many as thirteen field sparrows have, on historic occasions, populated the slab at once. After the feeder was in place, Barkis and I went up to the Christmas tree lot through the path we have been cutting through the savage multiflora. This afternoon I wanted to try shape-pruning some of the trees that otherwise wouldn't have any chance of selling themselves if, as we may, we throw the lot open to "cut your own Christmas tree" customers this year. All seemed to be going well, with some satisfying instant successes on the ten-year-old white spruce, when I noticed that the sun was getting low, my arms were getting heavy and, most important of all, Barkis had disappeared. When she did not come to my call I had to gamble she had taken the thousand-foot winding path through the high pasture bramble all the way home. To my relief (I had no stamina left for going back to search in the chill twilight) and yet to my concern (she had made a big, daring decision of her own and operated independently of her master) Barkis was safe in the yard, chasing the cats.

Hair

Thursday, Nov. 30. Whether hair is a pride or a problem, nuisance or glory, a thing of natural beauty or a bothersome physiological anachronism depends on where and how it grows and on the whimsical fashion of the time. The one constancy is that hair is the most persistent and energetic extension of itself the body produces; it will, ghoulish legend says, defy the grave. It is this constancy of growth for the filament, keeping us in a daily race with an unruly part of ourselves, never slowing down for age as do other functions of the body, that poses a worry for the fixed-income retirement budget. The price of a cut for a real head of hair used to be forty cents. Now, when there are only fringes, it is $2.75. Luckily, for the fashion moment, wearing hair long is respectable. The pensioner can decide to pay $2.75 only once, instead of twice, a month. This can be an economy, but not a happy solution. Hair, one of the ceaseless problems of life on both sides of every family, is also the key to pleasures, like running thoughtful fingers through one's own, getting the pillowed scent from a lover's, or tousling a child's. In addition to playing its role in such pleasures, it demands of us those toilet routines which do so much to pull us through the day and week; it rewards and reinforces such therapy with confidential whispers to our self-esteem. There is also, back on the clear pleasure side, the experience of having a good barber with a wise touch fuss soothingly about one's head for a luxurious twenty minutes. That was what went wrong when, searching for retirement convenience and economy today, I found a new neighborhood barber whose fee is only $2.50. His price is right, but he proved to have a touch that made me wish I could afford to go back to him every third day.

The Embarrassment of Not Being Poor Enough

Friday, Dec. 1. Although this is supposed to be the time of life in which society shows some special solicitude for our welfare, one thing does not change. In this retirement existence we still find ourselves in that unhappy zone of forgotten people who are not rich enough to afford the obligations of our position in life but not poor enough to get the help we could use. Once more, as it used to be with the college scholarships we vainly sought for our children, there is help we could use but can't get because mere statistics say we don't qualify. In college tuition days we went through the embarrassing ritual of detailing our modest financial circumstances not only to college authorities but to the friends whom we used as references in an effort to get some kind of scholarship aid for children who were qualified scholastically. Always there was the same result; our income, which did not seem to us capable of putting two children through college at the same time, was always, statistically, too high to qualify for assistance. The world was either for the very rich or the very poor, in college expenses as in medical expenses; the forgotten people in between would often face desperate struggle but never get help. One of the big questions we face in this retirement experiment of ours is whether we can afford to live in our own home, on which taxes have now multiplied to over fourteen times what they were when we began ownership. Yesterday was the last day for people over sixty-five to apply, at the town assessor's, for the special thousand-dollar reduction in assessment the Legislature recently enacted. I made the pride-sacrificing decision to go down and apply, only to discover, when I got to the fine print, that I would have to swear to a poverty more extreme than I could document. If we were just a little poorer we might be a lot better off. Where is the ingenuity and the heart of modern man and all his social planners, that such a situation should be so repetitive?

The Great Retirement Sin

Saturday, Dec. 2. You have to be careful to hold to the disciplines you have set for yourself. You must never let yourself stop to ask if it really makes any difference whether or not, for instance, you get up at the same time every retirement morning. To the cosmos, such a flit-speck time-space concern may be a nothing. To you, and to those around you, it is crucial. What may be hard to prove in relation to any particular morning is self-evident in the long-range sense. Start yielding a few moments with this or that excuse for one special morning and soon there will be a permanent alteration in the content of all mornings. And that is the first step into the greatest of all retirement sins, that of filling the day more and more easily with less and less. This week, after being out late at the theater, it was easy to sleep over half an hour. Another morning, when it was dark and snowing outside, fifteen minutes did not seem to matter. But this morning, frightened and full of resolution again, I forced myself — assisted by a clear light showing in the east — out of bed at 6:32, a normal pre-retirement schedule. Once the effort had been made it felt good, again, to be up and out of dismal undisciplined sloth. I will not, I tell myself, lie abed again. I hope to keep all the other therapeutic and antiseptic disciplines I have set myself, like the morning shower — whether I need it or not — and the dressing as if for occupation or sallying forth, even on days when I am not going anywhere I will be seen, and the regular hours, even if some of them are blank or would better have been, at this typewriter. If I do have a real zone of weakness it seems to be located, so far, in the siesta. It has extended itself slyly until it is sometimes close to an hour and a half instead of the forty-five minutes it used to be. And it is, on some of these windy early winter afternoons, harder to get up from.

Operation Christmas Tree

Sunday, Dec. 3. This should be the year when the private enterprise brand of old age security we tried to plant in these acres of ours begins to pay off. Twelve years ago we began, and continued for the next eight years, a program of planting between one and two thousand Christmas tree seedlings every spring. For several seasons drought held growth back; this is the first year in which our earliest plantings are ready for customers. But before we begin anticipating our profits we have to face up to a financial report on the Christmas tree venture to date. For three seasons past, there have been scattered trees of usable size. In these three seasons, twenty-one trees have left the place. Three were stolen; the other eighteen were gifts to various neighbors and friends. In some instances, if we had not given a Christmas tree, we might have spent money for some other kind of gift. But the hard economic fact lurking in the background is this: so far, after twelve years of work and growth, the plantation which was to provide an element of security in our old age has not put a single actual dollar bill into our pockets. In three years, I have succeeded in giving away eighteen trees and having three stolen; the circumstance for selling a single tree has not yet presented itself. As for the here and now, I just spent another afternoon up in the most accessible planting, trying to neaten things up for what is going to be, this year, some kind of effort to sell trees on a come-and-cut-your-own basis at five dollars a tree. Way back in the original planting days, we used to think of ten thousand trees at five dollars a tree and that was $50,000 in old age fortune. We have come far enough, already, to know that the real arithmetic is not going to be anything like that.

Pills

Monday, Dec. 4. Ours is a civilization of pills. We take them for every misery, real and imaginable. They have their own shelf in every home, their nook in every desk. Some of us organize our day into a timetable for taking them. Commercials for them dominate and standardize a large portion of our predominant cultural institution. The smaller the pill the more powerful and important its intended influence on the critical life processes of the body; the more of a jumbo it is, the more likely it has been designed not for hard, deep infighting with germs, virus, or the deteriorations of age, but for a shallower effect on the mind or on some of the more gullible nerves leading to it. The placebo, which provides nothing for something, is considered a legitimate and ethical variation. The taking of pills is attention to self, reaffirmation of ego and, at the same time, sharing in a great common experience. To frighten ourselves badly we need only imagine a world without pills, with mankind helpless and hopeless against all its physical and mental self-concerns. The other extreme — the possibility we might fall into a complete dependence on the pill as a way of life — doesn't frighten us as much as it should. It should appall us that we might succeed in finding contentment in pills alone. But we worry only about supply. Let our suddenly fallible economic system, which has been miscalculating in so many other fields lately, beware of blundering into an exhaustion of raw materials or a deficiency in manufacturing or distributing capacity; the dictionary finds a subliminal relationship between pill, the unpleasant-tasting dosage, and pillage, an unpleasant violence loosed on a whole scene.

When I stopped work, I was afraid pills might become a crutch I depended upon to make the days go round. I was concerned too, with any penny expenses that could raise dollar havoc with our budget. One thing I did was cut anti-arthritis pills from three to one a day, reducing the cost from thirteen and a half cents a day to four and a half. I take a little white pill for deep, vital work inside me, which costs a cent and a half a day. When I cut down on anti-arthritis pills, I was counting on the beneficial anti-arthritis side effect I discovered the moment I first took Vitamin C for a cold. I average fifteen hundred milligrams of Vitamin C a day. But I now buy it in a new drug store at half the price I had been paying, which cuts the daily cost from eight to four cents. The routine pills of my existence now cost ten cents a day as compared to twenty-three cents last August. That saves ninety-one cents a week, or $47.32 a year.

Our Mark on the Place?

Tuesday, Dec. 5. During the night there was a sleet and ice storm that left the trees and wires heavily coated, with trees bending down. During the day, when temperatures were supposed to rise and sleet was supposed to turn to a dwindling rain, there was a light, invisible drizzle that fused-froze itself to the existing ice. In mid-afternoon, here and there, the increased weight of ice became more than the wood could bear. Down came, section by section, the great white lilac which was, when we planted it, a thin sapling, but which had now, for many years, bloomed mightily by the kitchen door. It had been one of our own marks upon the place. Across the driveway there cracked down one of the sweeping lower branches from the maple that had been our first great transplanting triumph. Thirty years ago it had taken all four members of the family to carry its twenty-foot trunk down from the woods on the other side of the hill. Miraculously — maples, in reality, are celebrated for such miracles — it lived for us, until, now, it stands taller than the house, and has moments of spring beauty when it is like a poem breathing over us. On the other side of the house, across the brook, the gray birch we planted and which has delighted us by living far beyond its birch life span, is bent all the way down to the earth, and it is almost too much to hope that the bow it makes does not contain an irremediable split. Down by the pond, the sixty-foot willows we planted by driving small log cuttings into the moist shore look, from as close as we can bear to go today, as if they have lost half their branches. All these marks on the place, put where they were by the young family vigor with which we began our life here, are now gone or terribly scarred, and it is quite obvious that, when one ice storm undoes the plan and work and care of a lifetime, that is a kind of final verdict which we have no power to fight against. The story of our presence on this land is ending before we are. We have to clean up the mess and then decide if there is anything else we can do, or want to do.

Pre-Christmas Blues

Wednesday, Dec. 6. I sincerely hope that what I set down here on this subject is merely a highly unusual and highly personalized feeling. I hate to think there may be other human beings who are as dehumanized as the anticipation of our season of joy makes me feel and act. Today, out of a sense of schedule and duty, I went out of my way to spend a little time in a bookstore, looking for possible Christmas gifts. It was while I was in the store, walking slowly up and down the rows of shelves with a vacant feeling on my face and unseeing eyes in my head, that the terrible reality hit me. Here I was, in a store that sells my prime idea of what is a good possession, or the best kind of gift — the book, a product of the thought and genius and talent and spirit and love and any other emotion or experience of which human beings are capable. And yet the truth about me, judging by my thoughts and my behavior, was that what should have been an expedition of interest and delight was, instead, a disagreeable chore. Browsing was once, in imagination at least, a most pleasant way to spend an odd hour or two. But in early December being in a bookstore is like being inside a trauma, a dull, unfeeling, uncurious experience condemned to futility. Although vague memories from the book reviews during the past twelve months would suggest there must be many suitable gift titles hiding somewhere for anybody who really cared enough to find them and see them when he had found them, I recognized nothing I wanted to buy for anybody. I would not wish such an experience on anybody else, and I would not wish another human being such as I on the world. If I can't change I ought to crawl off somewhere by myself and stew in my own ugly, unfeeling juices until the rest of the world has had its good, unspoiled season of love.

The Old Gray Birch

Thursday, Dec. 7. The odds against recovery for the birch bent low by the ice storm of Monday and Tuesday were tremendous. Thirty years ago we transplanted the young birch, hoping it would be the son or daughter of a clump of white birches halfway up our hill. It turned out to be not a white birch, but a gray, shortest-lived of trees. We have had it on borrowed time for several years. It seemed to be in some kind of special performance, just for us, that it kept alive as long as it did and grew to a height of thirty feet. Yesterday morning it was bent all the way over in a long, giant bow, its top frozen fast into the meadow grasses.

And we were too heartsick to go close and encounter the death split which, we were sure, must have opened somewhere along the trunk. But late yesterday afternoon, when we came home from a Christmas shopping expedition, and heavy rains had begun to free the landscape from its case of ice, the tip of the old gray birch had somehow lifted itself off the meadow floor. Just before dark a strong wind came up, heaving the still half-prostrate tree up and down, but always, in our imagination, leaving it a little higher. Then, this morning, the birch was as tall and as straight as ever, a miracle of supple survival. Now this is not a diary for moralizing, and it may be remembered that the entry here only two days ago was one of somber admission that trees, like puppies, do not always match the human life spans with which they are associated. But if that old gray birch, already far past its normal life expectancy, already in its grace years, could take such an onslaught and then come out of it standing as tall and graceful as ever, ready for next spring's tender, sylphid greens as if its life were just beginning, if it could ease itself all the way back into its own beautiful posture after having been bowed all the way down to meadow muck, then what is this old gray life of sixty-five going to feel and think — what but a surge of fierce resolve and desire to have some more life, some more stand-up life, before its limbs are cased in cold!

The Checkbook

Friday, Dec. 8. This evening, working in the mundane choredom of the checkbook, I experienced a luxury I never could afford during the years of earning income. I paid all my bills in full. It is now a matter of survival necessity that all bills be handled as they come due; the retirement budgeteer cannot run the risk of letting even his telephone bill attain two months' growth before he handles it. No account can ever be given a chance to increase itself. It must be snuffed out, with payment, as soon as it appears. The result is that, once every month, after check-writing night, there comes a virtuous village blacksmith feeling, a moment when I owe not any man. It was never this way when I had my full earning power. Then the problem was always one of which bills could be reduced, by how much, and which could be put off, for how long. Now, once every month, I am solvent and free. I think that, as a result, I am beginning, for the first time, to have a really affectionate feeling for my checkbook. Where it once was the root residence of trouble and trauma, the nasty convenience that carried the high price of letting some inhumane institution know all the secrets of one's life, the pointless temptation to poor arithmetic, it now provides the monthly immersion by which one cleanses one's self of the sin of debt. After this ritual is completed, every month, the reading that is left is, for us retirees, the crucial barometer that tells us just how we stand in our battle for dollars and cents survival. Perhaps I should love the checkbook less if now, after the third monthly session, it were not holding up as well as it is. And I find it hard to forgive it for all those years when, with so much more money being poured in, it never once gave me the owing-not-any-man feeling. Nevertheless, here it is, when I need it most, behaving beautifully.

Winter Weather, Winter Soul

Saturday, Dec. 9. The old gray birch, prostrate last Wednesday, miraculously tall and straight again on Thursday, was bending again today under another ice storm. I sat in my window watching the freezing rain, watching the birch crown begin to droop again. That wonderful feeling which came with the recovery of the birch on Thursday began to yield before the accursed insistence and capacity of the coming winter. It can make a dozen such storms if it wishes. Today it relented. By mid-afternoon the storm had softened and the birch was straight and elegant again. But what is inside me didn't, this time, snap back as quickly as the tree. There is, along with the persistent closing in of winter weather, a winter of the soul. Here, only two days after being exhilarated by the example of the birch, I am demoralized by a feeling that this is getting to be a losing battle, after all — that the lows are going to get lower and longer, and the capacity to snap back weaker, until I am ready to sink down and bow my once foolishly proud crest in the admission that life defeats me. There has been excitement and stimulus in these first three months of the new existence, because so many new routines and circumstances were being instituted and adjusted to. But how will it be if the new illusions produce no more than the old? Such thought and feeling, on such a day, reveal how often weather is barometer to the state of mind.

Defying the Puritan

Sunday, Dec. 10. K arrived early this Sunday morning to cut a table Christmas tree for her apartment. She and Barkis and I walked through the mist and the wet until we both agreed we had found the tree she wanted. This was a good kind of walk, one K and I have taken many times in the course of our life on this land. She and I have often worked together with a maximum of wordless cooperation and a minimum of friction. It is pleasant to have her come back to the land for some of its yield. Aside from that early morning sortie, however, this has been a lost day. The Sunday papers were full of must reading, including reviews of two books in which the Rostow brothers are still trying to prove they were right about Vietnam.

Before I had myself clear for my stint at the typewriter it was time for lunch. After lunch there was football available, and today, for the first time in this new existence, I surrendered myself back to it. After football I tried to work a little, in the early evening. But all I was really doing was waiting for the Sunday evening whodunits, "The FBI," "Mannix," "The Protectors," to set themselves up for me. They finished a day completely non-productive except for that early morning walk through the wet with K. Are football and whodunits, therefore, a time-wasting addiction of which I should be ashamed? Tonight I find myself feeling bold toward that nosy, bossy Puritan who cohabits me. I claim the right to waste an afternoon and evening, and to waste it comfortably and warmly, if it so pleases me, inside the warm nullity of television.

The Mail

Monday, Dec. 11. In that nostalgic national yesterday of ours the delivery of mail was the only thing — except for counting us every ten years, taking us to war every forty years, and offering us a chance to vote for a President — that the federal government did for us. The mailman is still the one person who is good enough and kind enough to pay daily attention to the individual American. At the age of eleven I began taking advantage of the postal system by sending self-addressed envelopes out into the world of magazines, thereby guaranteeing myself some form of response. Ever since, the day's mail has been key to the day's mood. The first, the most important thing, the breath of life itself, is to get something. It is better to get bad mail, cruel, discouraging mail, than to get none at all. For the first few weeks of this new existence the mail was wonderful. There were surprising letters from surprising people who took surprising notice of the change in my fortunes. I myself, in that first burst of energy for looking for new horizons, sent out much more mail than usual, and it was responded to. It began to seem that something new and wonderful was about to happen every single day. It is hard to realize, now, after all those tingling weeks of high anticipation, that no sudden stroke of good fortune has arrived after all. But the mailman still comes every morning, and usually leaves something, and that, even though it is routine, does more than any other single factor to zip one day along after another.

How to Fail in Business Without Trying

Tuesday, Dec. 12. Once more I seem, with a certain perverse smugness I rather like in myself, about to prove that I am not a captain of industry, or a great merchandizer, or even one who is very hungry to harvest dollars from his own labor and enterprise. This should be the year we begin to sell Christmas trees. The progress report to date — Christmas is now two weeks from yesterday — is that the front portion of one field has been shape-pruned. It must also be reported, not necessarily as progress, that three trees have been cut: one the table tree for K, another full size for Miss P., delivered and set up in her parlor — both of these transactions in the realm of affection and not commerce — and a third brought down to the house during the snow squall this afternoon. This has now been put in a standard, and C has made a sign, "Cut Your Own $5," to hang on it, and it is ready to go out to the front driveway to entice whatever trade there may be. But tomorrow, unfortunately, we have our tickets to a play in Hartford so the tree and its sign cannot very well go out until Thursday. We have also accepted an invitation to brunch on Sunday, which would logically be the big rush day for

Christmas trees, if there is any rush here. Perhaps, by that time, we will have discovered, from some total lack of customers on Saturday, that there is no reason for us to give up the brunch. We will see what we will see and we will sell what we will sell, but I can think of all kinds of merchandizing anybody with a real knack for this sort of thing would have had going weeks ago. I believe I have a natural talent for not making money.

Snow

Wednesday, Dec. 13. To the snows of yesteryear and to those of these later years one part of us, the aesthetic rather than the corpuscle component, makes the same response. Snow is, first of all, a process in alchemy by which one known quantity in nature is converted into another, and the wonderful visibility of this process, falling across dark trees and red barns and green streetlights, together with its infinite variability — like the wave of the ocean and the cloud of the sky and the flicker of a log fire, it is ceaselessly never the same from one moment to another — makes watching it an addiction that will not let one go. As with all these other exponents of inexhaustible resource and freedom in pattern and motion, the first gift of falling snow — against all the realistic logic that thinks about driveways, hills, or the state of a family larder — is a gift of an hypnotic peace to the spirit. When it threatens to shut one in, the style of containment it involves also promises security, all rooted in folklore romance — ''Twas the Night Before Christmas,'' ''The First Snowfall'' and ''Snow-Bound'' — which begins in nonage, when snow is never anything but friend, and survives through the later years, in which snow sometimes becomes a blockage and a chore. All of which is this diary's way of acknowledging, safe inside its office and still far from the weight of a shovel or the spin of a tire, that there is a snow world this morning. The flakes slant across the window in droves, aimlessly, endlessly. Some day it will keep on and on and the spell never be broken.

A Sale

Thursday, Dec. 14. This morning, hung with the green and red lettered sign C had made, the Christmas tree went out to the mouth of the driveway. I watched for a while from the front window to see if people were at least looking at the sign. Everybody drove by as swiftly as usual, eyes unbelievably concentrated only on the road. I left the window for typewriter, for lunch, and then siesta. I had trouble getting a nap; once, when I had slipped off for a moment, I thought someone had been knocking at some door. When I emerged from my attempt at siesta, C made joyous proclamation: "I just sold a tree!" A "nice young man," with his wife and two children, had stopped. He was now up in the lot, seeing if he would find a tree he liked. How disappointing it would be, we both thought out loud, if our first customer couldn't find the tree he wanted! How horrible if he weren't "nice" after all, and might be capable of desecrating the holy season by cutting himself a beautiful tree and then driving off without bothering to come down and pay for it. The unworthy suspense on our part was soon ended. The young man and his family were back in the driveway. C went out and completed her transaction by taking their five-dollar bill and listening to their praise for the "perfect" tree they had found. It was the first five dollars from an enterprise which had begun twelve years before. There were no more customers today, but maybe the really nice young man will tell his friends what a wonderful place for perfect Christmas trees he has found.

Gifts Retirees Can't Afford to Get

Friday, Dec. 15. Please, all kind and thoughtful people, take second and third thoughts about that motorcycle which, the moment it popped into your heart, seemed just the right thing for you to give to your pensioner relative or retired employee. Devote this second and third look to an examination of whether this gift is going to involve an expense of any kind, like gasoline, insurance, or helmet, for the person to whom the gift is being made. You weren't going to give your Golden Ager a motorcycle? Here are two more realistic samples of gifts trailing expenses. One, most welcome last fall, was a camera I had been wanting for a long time, so I could take color pictures of the flower arrangements C makes. I hadn't used a camera in years, so I practiced with the first film cartridge. It took a five-dollar bill just to get the pictures back, let alone new film and new flash cubes for further operation. So I will be wondering, now and then, whether I can afford the next picture. How ridiculous! Now for the second example: The management from whom my separation last September was coolly amicable decided yesterday to make good on an early hint it might give me my desk, a huge semicircle built to my own special design. The desk itself was a gift, but I had to arrange to have it delivered. In order to get it into this room, the delivery men had to take it apart. The bill for trucking, dismantling, and then reassembling the desk was extremely reasonable, only thirty-five dollars. Yet it was thirty-five dollars for which I had made no calculation, and thirty-five dollars which, once taken out of the retirement nest egg, is never likely to be put back. These are two wonderful gifts, each something I wanted very much. To be honest, I am glad the donors never really did pause to calculate whether I could afford them. Yet, now that I have my camera and my desk, the point is firm: there are some gifts some people in some circumstances can't afford to get.

To You Coming After

Saturday, Dec. 16. Entry after entry, day after day, reveals this diarist totally wrapped up in the narrowing perceptions of his own particular station in life. Has he nothing to offer except this gossipy exchange of pensioner experience with other "Golden Agers"? Is this the most that life is about — to get this far, and then play the last few innings of the game from a contemplative wheel chair? What if there stumble into this diary some younger people not looking for pensioner experience, but drawn by love or curiosity to see what it may be like, between these covers? Has the old man nothing to say to or for them? Yes, indeed, all you who are coming after, and here is a slice of it. One of the sweet sadnesses very high in the feeling of all us older ones is that of a worried affection for all the younger people who are still strung out in the struggle along the path, who do not know their ending, or how they are going to make it. Every birth that comes after one is at once a miracle and a cruelty; one rejoices in the new life; one anticipates the sorrow the innocence thus born must inevitably encounter. One has to feel guilty, some of the time, for ever having helped bring anybody into this sadistic world. So I, the diarist, am sad for all you younger people, the ones I know and love and those I merely observe, and I have this wish for all of you, that life may be as kind to you as it can, and that you all, for your part, may be as kind to one another as you can. I wish mercy upon you all, and joy that is seasoned with proportion and sense so it won't decay on you, and I beg of you not to expect too much happiness from any source. At the same time I fiercely enjoin you not to be too cautious in guarding yourself against those moments of beauty and tenderness, or those instincts for perceiving potential nobility and dignity in the human behavior, which keep lingering on from your childhood. You have to learn to take all things together, layering and reflecting one upon another, compensating, marrying, conserving, spending, juggling, borrowing — and never take any final verdict from either evidence or experience but keep playing the possibility that some day, if you are lucky, you may end up loving and wishing well to the humanity in everybody. You may then discover that however you audit the human experience, it somehow manages to come out a plus, too, like people. Run along, now, to your young busyness, to your terrible maturity, to your first blank awarenesses of the end, but with your options of the spirit always open, to whichever of the ages of man is next for you.

Business Is Fun

Sunday, Dec. 17. A day or two ago, I was convinced that the business of selling was something quite foreign to my nature. A day later, on the wings of the sale of the first Christmas tree, I was admitting the pleasure of hearing a young couple praise the beauty of the tree we had grown while they handed over five dollars for it. Tonight, on the basis of eight sales yesterday and eight more today, I am strutting about (or sitting in an ostentatious frown of high calculations) as if I were an assured success in the world of finance, enterprise, and commerce. This is an inflated touch of euphoria, especially when one realizes how far from ten thousand trees at five dollars apiece the score for this first season — seventeen — now stands.

213

Nonetheless, the feeling is wonderful. The eighty-five dollars in hand happens to be just enough to adjust my December budgeting back toward solvency. But — and this observation may restore and reinforce my original admission that I am not for this kind of success — the real return from these sales has not been the price. It has been the voluntary tributes the customers have given to the trees we have grown. It has been the light and love in the faces of the very young couple who were so obviously about to have their first Christmas together. This was the direction from which the euphoria descended, euphoria composed of the wonderful feeling that we and our land had produced something that was fitting into what was going to be a beautiful moment in the lives of some other people. We took their five-dollar bills in a mutual exchange of happiness. We almost gave the money back, as if there could be no possible sense or profit in taking it, to the one customer who grumbled that he hadn't been able to find just what he wanted but had taken one that "would do." Is selling happiness a business? Don't we hear some high-pressure sales manager telling his crews that, of course, it is the very best kind of business, and the reason they have been provided with the world's best vacuum cleaner?

The Other Presence

Monday, Dec. 18. The other presence in this house is, as has been noted, a vaunted operator of the vacuum cleaner and an eloquent proprietor of the telephone. But today, not for the first time in this new existence, I discovered something more about C and something more about myself. This was another of those days when C went out for lunch with one of her groups, leaving me to my own devices. Both she and I have, I imagine, nourished what we considered secret illusions to the effect that the man likes to be left alone occasionally, sole lord of the manor. Possibly both of us have calculated, too, that such an occasional separation of days might be especially healthy now that we have entered the retirement style of life, with the greatest part of both our lives, for the first time, centered within the same four walls, day after day. But today, hour by hour, I began to notice the truth. I kept listening for the familiar moves around the house. I found it frustrating that I couldn't wander out of my office and manage a casual encounter. I missed the regular morning intrusion when C watered, or pretended to be watering, the rosemary plant on my office table. Although our lunches are seldom talkative, they are never empty of communication and feeling; today's was the most perfunctory sandwich I have ever consumed. The house was not only empty; all the touches she had left behind were, without her own presence to give them warmth and light and animation, mere tantalizers rather than comforts and reassurances. It wasn't until nearly four in the afternoon that she finally came home and turned the house, and life, back on.

A Tree for Us

Tuesday, Dec. 19. After all those singing moments, over the weekend, when we reveled in the way the customers came back full of praise for the beauty of the Christmas trees we had raised on this place, we ourselves, today, went up to get our own tree. There is a perennial family dispute, polite but deep, over the size of the tree, with C the advocate of the small, slim shape, and the rest of us in favor of some degree of opulence. This was the year for C to have her choice. Still, it was my duty to present, by finding a handsome sample, the case for the big tree so that her final selection would have to be between the best of both possible styles. The difficulty we encountered soon after we had begun walking through the rows of white spruce was that we did not seem to have any very good trees in either slims or fats. There was something wrong — some break in symmetry, some lack of fullness on one side or at the top — with every single tree we stopped to consider. We wandered aimlessly and with a growing chill in our hands and feet from the cold, damp afternoon until finally, with C's desperate permission, I put saw to a tree that looked like a compromise, relatively young and short, but nicely full. The moment we had it back at the house and held it up inside we knew it was not a tree either of us wanted. We went back to the lot and cut the really slim one she had looked at indecisively before, and brought it back through the dusk, with our hands and feet strangely warm this time. We set it up and discovered that those customers had been right, after all, and that we did grow beautiful Christmas trees.

Cards

Wednesday, Dec. 20. During the years when we could afford it we had little interest in sending out Christmas cards. We did so on only two occasions, once when the first two children made a dewy picture coming down a flight of stairs in nightgowns, carrying candles, and later, after we had moved into this house, when an itinerant etcher had put it on a card for us. Otherwise we have never put out. Our failure to play the game has meant our gradual elimination from the lists maintained by people who periodically check receipts against outgo. We never seriously considered forcing our way back into the system by mailing out cards of our own again. To the contrary, as the quality and design of the cards themselves seemed to grow cheap and garish over the years, it seemed a good thing to be out of. We were grateful to those few fast friends who kept remembering us even though we never carded them, and that was that. This year, as though to torment us both in the realm of conscience and that of taste, there has been not only a slight increase in the number of cards coming to us but a spectacular improvement in their quality. No single one has been lurid; most have been simple and beautiful in design, like the Christmas cards of childhood, and they make, without any of the sorting usually necessary, a splendid display on the mantel. For the first time in many years, but a little late to do anything about it, we are wondering how it would feel if we were the kind of people who would put time and effort and thought and a little cash into the business of sending out, to others, the kind of card we like to get ourselves. What is this life all about, anyway, that we are too busy, or too unthinking or uncaring, or too intent on saving petty cash for something else, to be like other nice people and play our own part in this ritual of thoughtfulness? Right now, if we could have instant cards out in this year's mail, we probably would. Will we make next year's mail? That, knowing ourselves as we do, is the real question.

Sentimentalia

Thursday, Dec. 21. Going through the odd piles of old letters, programs, vacation bills which had to be cleared and filed if my new home office combination of semicircle desk and old mill room table is to be given a bare, clean start, I came again and again today to items I hardly knew were there and yet could hardly bear to throw away. In the final disposition I followed no set rule, but did find myself keeping two things in mind. One was that there would not be many more times for me to go through this collection of memorabilia, so I ought to begin getting rid of some of it. The other was that I had an obligation to think, not what these items might mean and say to me, but what they might mean and say to others who would, some day, have the chore of looking at them and deciding what to do with them. By such a consideration, for example, one threw away, at last, the two bittersweet letters in which a daughter had first misunderstood one's conduct and then, in her next, found all clear and happy again, and ended the misunderstanding. If one found four letters from a dear friend, one sacrificed two at this time, to lighten the task for whoever would have to take the final look through the file. Some of the fan mail from the past, while still beautiful, had lost importance. And so I, who am the one who never wants anything to end, not even pain, not any part of life, have been sitting here most of the day, lopping off and throwing away to where they will never awaken my sentiments again, those pieces of paper which mean so much more to me than they could possibly mean to anyone else. It is a little like cutting off an arm and throwing it into the fire, never to be used again. Goodbye. Goodbye dear moments, dear but not so dear I can't forget them, once the tangible evidence has been cast out.

Slipping out of the Midstream

Friday, Dec. 22. Yesterday in this space I was waxing sentimental about throwing away the evidential reminders, old letters and old clippings, of some of my yesterdays. Goodbye, goodbye, I said, with sweet sorrow, again and again. Today, in a curious contraincidence, I found myself considering the possibility of a less sentimental farewell to the lifestyle I followed during work and career. I went downtown for the Friday luncheon which was regular habit for the last fifteen of those years and which has survived into this new pensioner phase.

Today, for the first time, I began to feel a real separation between that old world, with its meshed-gear urgencies, and my own new routines of less activity and involvement. It was not merely that the restaurant was full of special pre-Christmas groups, each united by payroll as well as by sentiment. It was that, for the first time, I had the feeling that my own good friends and luncheon companions had a traction and momentum and direction in their lives to which I and my new existence had little connection and in which I was beginning to have some slight trouble maintaining an interest. I felt like a boat edging out of midstream in toward some quiet lagoon where the pull of the current and the stroke of the wind are not quite so strong and where, with less struggle, one has more chance of having one's way about something, providing it is a modest something. It was still a little sad to feel a distance opening between those in the race and the one beginning to drop quietly out of it, and perhaps some Ulysses part of one still felt a vain twinge of muscle that thought it wanted to be back out there, smiting the furrows again. But on balance it felt good. This is no reflection upon, or discouragement to, those whose age and vigor and circumstance keep them still in the race. Perhaps, better than I ever did, they know where they are going, and why.

The Customer

Saturday, Dec. 23. The twenty-second cut-your-own Christmas tree customer was different. He parked out in the road instead of entering the driveway. He came to the front door instead of the more- and easier-traveled-to side door. And he wore a black skin. His knock at the door caught me back in the conditioning I had grown up in rather than in the sophistication I thought I had been achieving during these recent years when

I have known and written that our very survival depends upon our success in meeting and solving the race issue. To have the first black customer was a strange experience and I examined him as if he were a curiosity, as if wearing glasses and a studious look had a special distinction when skin was black — as if, in fact, his wanting a Christmas tree had something questionable about it. When he had gone up to the lot, I went to the window and strained my vision in that direction, somehow expecting to find his black face stand out against the background of white snow. After he had come down with his tree, and paid for it, and driven off into America, my sense of strangeness in the transaction shifted toward a warm and pleasant feeling. It had become, suddenly, a bigger, more inclusive Christmas.

More Color

Sunday, Dec. 24. Yesterday it was a black Christmas tree customer. Today it was a green bird. It made its appearance during the morning, on the crab-apple tree, out the green window of the green plant room. Vivid parrot green, with ornate head and sweeping tail, it obviously was one of those birds always making radio programs and want ads columns which sometimes arrange their capture and safe return to their home cages. Today, Christmas Eve, would have been fitting for a Good Samaritan operation but for that no one quite had the energy. Instead we merely lavished upon the bird the excessive attention we human beings instinctively give to a color that is different. This was another pigmentation which, being obviously native to some tropical jungle, seemed out of place against a background of New England snow. Yesterday we strained our eyes up toward the Christmas tree lot, calculating that our black customer would show up so well against the snow background we could watch him and see how he was doing. Today the green bird was more cooperative, flying from the plant room crab-apple tree to the living room lilac, as if mocking, while condescendingly cooperating with, such provincial human beings who never seemed to have seen real color against snow before. Then, this evening, one of our guests had firm information our bird was not anybody's parakeet but the descendant of the monk parrot, a brand which, a few years ago, had escaped from the slavery of a shipping cage in New York Harbor, and had, ever since, free as any native bird, been moving into Connecticut in increasing numbers. We will, in time, get accustomed to the monk parrot, too.

The Carol

Monday, Dec. 25. About three o'clock in the afternoon, some four hours after the business of opening the presents had been finished and just after the turkey had been taken out of the oven, transferred from its cooking pan to a platter and then put back in the oven, our group of voices, some of which had come to sound cracked with age, found itself around the piano, some of whose keys were out of tune, belaboring the old group of carols. Rashly ambitious, at first, for all of them, but at ease, actually, only with "Silent Night," and then, alas, only with the first verse, which half of us kept repeating while the other half pressed on, we came to a not totally unexpected moment, because similar moments had come in other years, when we suddenly held each other tightly around the waist, and clutched back tears, and felt our ears flooded and muffled as if we were trying to hear something under water, and knew that, almost against belief and hope, the moment that said to us that this was what it was all about, this was what made it all worthwhile and beautiful, that moment had come again, had come once more, had come one more time, had come to us all together one more time.

Hercules Gets Help from His Harem

Tuesday, Dec. 26. Remembering now, from the days of youth and from those of what is called the full vigor of manhood, I resurrect and reapply, even to me at my present age, the greatest single guiding law of New England life — perhaps, for that matter, of all life, everywhere: Whatever is necessary must also be possible. The merciless, unrelenting application of this creed took me, today, out to try to deal with the problem of a large branch which had begun to split off the front yard maple. If the branch were sawed off where it joined the trunk, its fall would endanger utility wires coming into the house, and might even threaten traffic on the road out front. The problem was to cut through the branch, part way up, and somehow induce it to settle down before it took its fall. It had to be done, therefore it had to be possible. And it had to be possible for me, not just for the tree surgeon whose fees for touching a tree begin at seventy-five dollars. Under this whip I, who begin trembling and feeling a strange muffled sensation around the heart when I go up over three rungs on a ladder, moved irresolutely into action, terribly uncertain of methods or results. After innumerable painful trips up the ladder I sawed the branch at fifteen feet above the ground. Instead of falling, it settled back on its own stump, sustained by the way its branches interlocked with those of the main tree. I took a sledge hammer up the ladder and, with timid, awkward strokes, eventually jarred the branch off its stump. It dropped straight down a distance of three feet, an important gain in the safety factor for its eventual fall. The problem now was to twist and free it for the remainder of its fall. I was frightened and acknowledging to myself that I would probably have to call a tree surgeon after all when the holiday houseful of women took over. SJ came out and suggested I tie a clothesline around the bottom of the floating branch to help pull and twist it into falling. We pulled in one direction and gained another foot of settle. Gesturing from the window, C suggested that we now pull from ninety degrees more to the south. That gained another two feet. Now K came out and insisted that we take our line due east and give it a pull. The branch crashed down beautifully, threatening neither wires nor road. The trembling Hercules had had his necessary feat accomplished, and no doubt his life saved, by the engineering tactics contributed by his three women. That old New England principle of life merely said that anything that was necessary was also possible. It never said it was always going to involve a glorious masculine triumph.

What the Hurry Is

Wednesday, Dec. 27. Immediately after
the holiday dedicated to the celebration of a
Birth, the business of death has taken over
and has been making its point with me more
effectively than ever before. Former
President Harry Truman began it, out in
Independence, Missouri, leaving at the age
of eighty-eight — an age which, being
twenty-three miraculous years away from
my own, constitutes no threat to me. But
while the media and the nation take the
death in Independence for their theme,
with only Mrs. Truman's magnificent
good sense restraining them from another
real orgy in ornate simulation of
sentiment, there are other obituaries in
the news which come closer in geography
and in age. People are dying all around

me at such an age as seventy, and when they die at seventy nobody acts as if this were at all unusual or unexpected. But seventy is, suddenly, a number only five removed from my own age. Is it only five more years, then, that I may have for everything I still want to cram into my life? For being nicer to people? For trying to do some one little thing that might be beautiful? For selling the Christmas trees I planted? For doing something more about seeing three grandsons, those very real young people, Alan, Chris and Troy, on the West Coast? For drawing more polluted air down this wheezy throat into these half-lesioned lungs? No wonder I feel, at that very stage of life when they say one is supposed and entitled to take it easy, as if I had never been in such a frantic hurry, with so many things to do in such cruelly little time.

On Being Nicer
to People

Thursday, Dec. 28. Yesterday, in the course of that wheedling plea for a longer life I was making, I pretended that one of the things I wanted time for was "being nicer to people." The implication was that I wanted to compensate, now I have reached the stage of pause and thoughtfulness, for some of the selfish, thoughtless and abrasive actions of those more pressured years when I acted first and regretted only if consequences began catching up with me and exacting some retribution from me personally. It is true that I would like to do something like this, if it could be neatly arranged, without too much real sacrifice or change on my part. My instinct to avoid any real sacrifice, such as might be involved in trying to make it up to some particular individual for some particular injury, is reinforced by a piece of advice from the field of child psychology, warning the parent who was still worrying, years later, about an injustice he had once committed against his child. The warning was that trying to square this mistake in some conspicuous way might do more damage than merely trying to forget it as old, closed business. Perhaps the child had not noticed or felt the injustice as much as the parent himself had. Perhaps, for the child, the event had been successfully scarred over. Perhaps the child would be more upset and embarrassed by some bumbling attempt to balance the books than he had been by any original action or inaction. This theory, at least provides a possible wisdom that coincides with my own instincts and with what may be the limit of my capacity. I want time to be nicer to people, not to try to go back and reopen and re-balance with beautiful deeds of atonement all those specific remembered acts of thoughtlessness and unkindness of which my conscience has such a full record. The best way to try to pay the world what I owe it and to deal with that mild nagging in my conscience (most active, I notice, in moments when I am thinking of my approaching encounter with an end of everything) is not to try to rework the past but to surprise the future with some fresh new decencies and kindnesses, not necessarily involving old scores or old relationships, not expiations or atonements for old sins, but free, unsigned contributions of positivities such as may astound, and hearten, those who may find them touching their lives. Having thus philosophized so comfortably, I now must pledge to record it here, if I ever, ever really manage such an act.

The Old Couple

Friday, Dec. 29. This noon we dressed ourselves up, I in a new and stunning Christmas shirt and tie, C in a black sweater very chic. We drove five miles to try a nondescript new restaurant for lunch. We ordered scallops and veal. C had one drink. We had no dessert. The cost was six dollars. We left the restaurant after forty minutes and drove home by a circular country route, stumbling upon and exclaiming over an extensive nursery plantation in which orderly rows of young yews and arborvitae and hemlock extended for acre after acre. We were out of the house altogether for less than two hours. We were highly dressed for no other reason than that we both felt it might be good to get out of the house and deliberately see and do something different; we were behaving exactly in the style of some of the well-known retired couples about town we used to watch with a mixture of admiration, wonder, and pity. We used to admire the way they kept up their immaculate appearance. We used to wonder how much forced and anguished pretense might go into their public masquerade of contentment and security. We used to pity them for the possibility that what really kept them on the move for such unimportant errands and time-killers was some cruel experience of loneliness and

238

boredom. We sometimes thought of them as lost souls, floating around in some Dantean stage of their existence, waiting to be released into the next. And now, today, there we were ourselves, behaving the same way, doing the same kind of thing, and perhaps creating the same mixture of response and speculation in the minds of any younger people who happened to notice us. What is our report, now, from this side of the age dividing line? First, it is possible for two people, who have long ago established their mutual assurances, to have a good time doing rather inconsequential things together. Second, yes, we probably did need some quick variation in routine, scene, and people to look at. We were looking for therapy, keeping up our own morale, rather consciously and deliberately dealing with the psychological needs of our position as a pensioner couple. Third, however, we need no sympathy and require no pity. There are, for people who have begun to come to terms with life, and with the end of life, Indian summer moments and moods and routines that have a mellow richness all their own.

Being Poor in Private Is No Pain

Saturday, Dec. 30. We decided, last September, there was no reason the rest of the world had to see, in our retirement life-style, any conspicuous adjustment to our reduced income. We might be poor but we would not act poor. We would, in the beginning at least, dress as well as ever. We would go more, not less often, to the theater. The economizing would be done, if possible, in our own privacy, where there would be no one to observe it. All this, translated into the grocery department for this holiday week, meant that we had the usual Christmas Eve ham and oysters and the usual size turkey the next day. And, since what goes under a

Christmas tree is in some degree a public display, there was no stinting there, either. That was five days ago. Since then we have been operating in privacy. Tonight we had a third go at the turkey, with mashed potato and turnip left over from the Christmas Day dinner. Next there will be a curry, which should be of a quantity for two more meals. We have dined twice on and made numerous sandwiches from the ham, which will go for two more dinners. To some degree we will even out that stupendous Christmas grocery bill, which was larger this year, because of higher prices for the same items, than anything we ever thought we could afford when I was working. The good point about this is that we like leftovers. We always did like leftovers. Rather than being one of the hardships of the pensioner life, they are one of its pleasures. It is no pain at all, being poor in private.

When a Junco Falls

Sunday, Dec. 31. I am not sure anybody from a higher altitude was watching and taking note, but I, from the dining room window, was a sympathetic witness this morning when a junco, not the more Biblical sparrow, slipped and fell. The junco slipped and fell, lying sprawled for a moment before it could use its wings to right itself, when it tried to run on the smooth glare of ice laid down by the freezing rain that began yesterday afternoon and lasted all night. The demonstration that conditions outdoors had become too treacherous even for a junco delivered a warm and comfortable message to me, the witness looking out through the window. It would be ridiculous to venture out and, under the new condition of my life, I was under no compulsion to try it. The fact that a small junco hop had ended up in an undignified sprawl for one of the earth's best masters of the arts of equilibrium was instant liberation from any conceivable demands the world outside might make on us, even including invitations to New Year's Eve parties, if we had happened to have any. We have the excuse for spending the festive evening snug at home, for drawing the curtains, for curling up with ourselves, for being comfortably alone, for behaving, while this weather lasts, as if we were in a state of partial hibernation. Once again the swiftness with which experience and mood and feeling revolve amazes me. Only two days ago we were busting out of here for a nondescript lunch any place, any place else, anything for a change of scene. Today, with the luxurious kind of shiver people give for a cold they do not have to go out into, we are drawing the same place close in around us and wrapping ourselves up in it.

Settling Day

Monday, Jan. 1. From somewhere in my reading — I cannot dredge it up as an actual experience memory from my boy's life in a Connecticut farm neighborhood — I picture the first of the year as a "settling day" when the farmers of a district went about balancing their accounts with one another. Three years ago, when I had let the year end without paying our last and only full-time-farmer neighbor for the mowing he had done for us, it seemed mere courtesy to drive over on New Year's Day, find him in his barn, and hand him the envelope that squared things between us for the start of another year. I found I liked the experience, and have since pretended it is a fixed custom. It is a good feeling to have one's bills paid. It is pleasant to contrive an old-fashioned

New Year's Day ceremony. Today we did this again, and after we had left off the envelope, C and I continued driving through the hinterland, pretending we had other calls to make. In the back of my mind, as we were enjoying this, there was the thought that this might be the last year we could afford even the one transaction we had completed. I now set down, in capsule form, the economic history of this farm-place of ours and its hay acreage. When we took title, thirty-one years ago, there were twenty acres in hay. The first few years we sold the hay standing for $125 plus several loads put into our own barn for our own use. The town tax on the place then was a hundred dollars a year. The hay paid our taxes, fed our cow, and gave us twenty-five dollars over. The present day statistics are these: Town taxes — $1,400; acres still in hay — 3; number of cows — 0; cost of getting the three acres mowed so it does not revert to brush — $25; total deficit, taxes and mowing together — $1,425. This was something one could afford, for sentimental, aesthetic reasons, when one was at work. It is more difficult trying to make it seem sensible, or possible, for a fixed low income. We may, next year, have to let the grass grow and the brush begin.

How Do You Get a Day Off?

Tuesday, Jan. 2. "In this retirement business," said a friend who had preceded us into it, "a holiday is just another day, like any other." That is the way it has been. The outside world ceases certain activities and shuts itself down; for us the red letters on the calendar do not seem to matter, the routines of our life carry on as usual. We sometimes experience twinges of annoyance because there is nothing we can suddenly stop doing just because everybody else is, quite irresponsibly, taking a day off. In the wake of this

Christmas - New Year's syndrome, the question has been thrusting itself sharply at us: How do we pensioners get a vacation from not having a job to go to? How do we get a holiday from routine? How do you contrive to take a vacation from a vacation? Should we seek, as one of the guaranteed benefits of our old age pursuit of happiness, the privilege of returning to a job for as many days a year as those still employed take holiday? How do we get away from it all, from the lack of responsibility, from the pressure of not having anything that has to be done, from the daily grind of our non-involvement?

Never Ask How They Are

Wednesday, Jan. 3. In the corridor crowd at the organization session of the new Legislature today a gentleman from another time and another city approached me and recalled old times. We were quite successful, between us, in calling up the names of people we had both known thirty-five years ago. That led to the particular anecdotage which now threatens, like the death of Falstaff babbling of green fields while the chill climbed his legs, to claim a permanent place in those thoughts that, at this time of life, always lie just beneath the surface, waiting their chance to leap out and terrorize us. "How's Nobby?" I asked, referring to a valiant associate of ancient poker and beer days and nights. "He died last February," the answer began. "He had quite a time of it. There was this trouble with circulation in his leg, and he wouldn't trust his own doctor, so his son got him a specialist up from New York. The specialist looked at him, before he put him to sleep, and said, 'I'll just have to take the big toe off, and that will be all.' Then, when Nobby woke up, they had taken it off at the knee. The surgeon had followed it all the way up from the toe, and there was nothing else he could do. It was all doomed. But you can imagine what that did to Nobby, and how he behaved when he realized what they had done to him." I found, as I stood listening, that I could imagine very well, partly because the leg I was standing on had a strange feeling of numbness, sometimes in the shin region. So long, Nobby. Sorry about the way it happened to you. Sorry, too, that I asked.

Braceland on Senescence

Thursday, Jan. 4. Dr. Francis J. Braceland, longtime head of the Institute of Living at Hartford, has been on the lecture platform with a discussion of the problems of "senescence" which, with optimistic bravado, he defines as "increase in years without deterioration and decay." Dr. Braceland's optimism is many-faceted. He finds, in us oldsters, only a "mild tendency to garrulity." He proclaims that "the old person yearns for, needs and desires the same satisfactions as the young, differing not in quality though somewhat in degree. Yet the culture has a bias against their expression. What is virility at 25 is lechery at 65. . . . Actually sex in later years correlates strongly with sex in earlier years. It is a timeless drive through life, even in the 80s and 90s." Dr. Braceland also rationalizes, and even offers to cure, our apparent forgetfulness. "Complexes which lead to forgetting," he contends with a cute reversal of direction for his logic, "are just as active in old age as they are in other periods of life. The forgetting of proper names is often due not to lack of interest, but also to the fact that the memory is repressed for some unconscious reason. There is definite difficulty in recall among this age group. It sometimes happens that old people are hospitalized because of disorientation, confusion and an apparent loss of retentive memory, looking for all the world as though serious organic brain changes are operative; yet under a program of attentive care and adequate stimulation, the failing faculties are soon restored." We feel a bit churlish as we question how much of Dr. Braceland's relatively cheerful wisdom can be reconciled with actual Golden Age experience. We wonder how many would agree that the major difference between sex at twenty-five and sex at sixty-five is what the "culture" calls it. We wish we could believe in some therapy that would catch and cure us when we are about to wax garrulous about ancient escapades to somebody whose name we can't remember. As it is, we suspect Dr. Braceland of having attained his counseling dotage, which is, like senility, another word for senescence.

The Seed Catalogue

Friday, Jan. 5. I hesitate to add one more to the millions of pieces written about the spring seed catalogue arriving in the midst of January winter. But this arrival, to this individual in this year, is not quite like all the others. This is the year when I am supposed to have all the time I really need to make precisely the kind and quality of garden I have always talked about. This is finally becoming that stage of life — the reminders keep accelerating and multiplying — when there is a limit to the number of gardens one is going to make. While I make gardens that classic rustic fellow with the scythe is also working the neighborhood. This year's, then, is going to be a garden especially worth planning in advance, worth fussing over, worth putting love and affection into. It is dangerous to commit one's self to this kind of effort. It is when people raise the stakes late in the game that the fates play their cruelest tricks.

Nonetheless the whole thing has to be risked. This is what life is about, or it is about nothing. The catalogue that came today is Robson's, from Hall, New York, and it is the particular catalogue to which I am already eternally grateful for Seneca Chief hybrid sweet corn, which tastes the way old-fashioned Golden Bantam is supposed to taste but doesn't, for my first introduction to the glories of Buttercrunch Bibb lettuce, the most elegant food ground can grow, and for the great gardening joy that has come with the cucumber named Burpless Hybrid, a nomenclature which concentrates on one possibly imaginary asset to the neglect of other tremendous virtues like strength of plant, rapidity and magnificence of yield, and above all, restoration or recapture of full and true cucumber flavor. I feel the moist earth now, and the sun, and the good summer sweat among the weeds (only there won't be any weeds this year) and all my flesh and blood is happy.

Getting Outdoors —
the Act of Will

Saturday, Jan. 6. This was the first day of the winter when the aging blood — only yesterday seed-cataloguing itself enthusiastically along the road to spring — had trouble just getting itself outdoors. There were great advantages in some of the circumstances of earlier life in this New England — the necessity for getting out to take care of a cow, the routine of the outdoor toilet, the insistent demands of the woodbox in the house and the woodshed outdoors. They were routine necessities which required that, no matter what the weather outside, one bundled up and got out there with something to do that encouraged deep breathing of the cold, clean air. It helped, as well, not to have hourly forecasts and discussions of the weather. Today, for instance, the professional weathermen were noticing that, in addition to a temperature of around twenty, there was a wind-chill factor that took it down to where it felt like minus fifteen degrees. With such coaching one could see the chill, strong wind blowing and nourish an excessive dread of going out into it. To get outdoors today took an act of will. Perhaps it was loyalty to the need of Barkis for some free running exercise that tilted the decision the right way. Once I had been out there for five minutes I knew once more, of course, that I must never fail to make it, not any single day. One reason is that if I ever let myself not make it, that would be the beginning of that sloth and fat and that lack of mind exercise and deep breathing which would be the swifter deterioration of the cadaver in which I live. The other and even more important reason is that there is, once you get out into it, nothing quite as lovely as a sharp winter afternoon, with the intimate, almost friendly and yet treacherous tickle of cold coming into the fingers and toes, and the air, the air, knifing its therapeutic surgical way into throat and lung and thought. The trouble is one does not always remember this until one has, once more, fought off a thousand persuasive inertias and forced one's self, once more, out into the ordeal that turns into tonic.

Start Going to Church?

Sunday, Jan. 7. Almost any of these pensioner Sundays there is likely to be a casual thought, no nearer a resolve than a slight candle is to a burning bush, about the possibility that I might, some day, now that I am getting near the end of the journey, decide to end it where it began — in the arms of a church. My last experience with certainty was when, back at the age of eleven, I went through the ceremony of being made a member of the church, with the assured rustle of guardian and eventually welcoming angel wings all around me as I stood up in the filtered sunshine of that lovely May morning. Now there is, as every honest pensioner is likely to admit to himself, some degree of possibility I might come to the mood and impulse in which, without believing in that certainty any longer and having had nothing but abrupt intellectual dismissal for it all these intervening years, I would head back and play my own intensive, demanding part in some re-creation of the holy charade. I could hate myself and have contempt for myself for doing it; I could also, possibly, understand and forgive myself. To have the good feeling of singing the old hymns once more. To sidle, unobtrusively, back into the recital of the Lord's Prayer. To deliberately let the preacher have my ear for twenty minutes a week, and to begin the tactful process, in return, of drawing him into such pleasantries as might establish his final twenty minutes with me, when I am in my casket, as an act of comradeship more than a professional duty. Who, after all, is going to say the words over me with a proper understanding of just what kind of bargain a sophisticated character like me could be capable of making with an organized religion? The beauty of it, of course, is that I do not need to go through any Canossan drama, no spectacle of reconversion. I could begin by going casually, once a month. Later I would resist, modestly, the suggestion that I get my letter for transfer of membership from the old church at Newtown. Leave the formal affiliation and running the church to the professionals who have been going to church all the years I haven't. Will I do it? Don't trust me not to. "Rock of ages, cleft for me." "One Sweetly Solemn Thought," the hymn my mother played and sang the night before she died when I was four years old. "Jesus, Lover." Wouldn't it be, considering the life I've led and the thoughts I've had, an obscenity? Ah, but what is one more final sin on the way to a possible forgiveness for them all?

Stars

Monday, Jan. 8. Night and day followed one another. The moon appeared and reappeared, repeating itself but in different orbits. Once every twelve moons there was a rotation of the seasons. Our first intelligence, wherever it arrived on this planet, must have discovered these elemental routines rather promptly, perhaps, in each instance, the first time around. But it may have taken that first intelligence more than one rotation of the seasons to begin to notice and then to chart and remember the fact that there was, overhead, a fixed firmament of stars which never changed their positions relative to one another and which, in their concerted movement, appeared and reappeared at certain times in certain places in the night sky year after year.

But this relatively sophisticated certainty, more complicated to notice and certify than night and day, the moon series, or the seasons, has probably contributed more to the stability of human expectation, more to the serenity and peace of the human mind, more to the development of the scientific quest, and more to the nourishment and replenishment of hope than any other discovery the human intelligence has made about its host universe. Certainty mixes with mystery, the laws of universal physics with the emotions of the blood, the sense of preordained destiny with the stretching out of a limitless future whenever we lose ourselves, for a moment, to the stars. I have always been going to fix the winding precisions of the stars so firmly in my own mind I could be an authority on them on any given night. I never make it: my feeling and emotion, on any given night, are not much ahead of those of the first intelligence that realized it had seen the stars repeating themselves. But that is enough; that first wonder has never faded.

The Great Misery

Tuesday, Jan. 9. It has, within the space of the last eighteen hours:

Turned the whole retirement experiment toward a melancholy, fateful feeling of stalemate and defeat.

Killed the flavor in that clear, cold winter air outside.

Driven the nostalgia out of memory.

Stifled anticipation.

Converted cats and dogs to pests instead of pets.

Made it difficult to believe anything can be really worthwhile — to think or to say or to try to do.

Shuttered the glory and beauty of a fresh moon in a brilliant setting of winter twilight pastels.

The one thing that can do all this, without much more than suggesting its own presence, is the cold — not necessarily just the old-style common cold, but even the modern Vitamin C cold, with its relatively restrained flows, congestions, and agues.

Today, even with such Vitamin C mercy in the touch of the first cold of the year, is the most non-livable day I ever hope to encounter. Nothing else but a cold can turn a whole world around like this. Television, for all its thoroughly dreary ingenuity in commercials, hasn't begun to probe its misery.

January

Wednesday, Jan. 10. The cold, the first retirement cold, continues — smothered down, it is true, by a continual gobbling of Vitamin C tablets, but the symptoms managing, nonetheless, to follow their accustomed sequence. It is a fact, perhaps dangerous and regrettable, that this retirement circumstance poses fewer necessities that have to be met and served no matter how one happens to feel. So what was always true to a great extent — that once a cold took hold no other activity except fighting the cold could really matter — applies even more conclusively now. Until the cold has begun to let go there is no routine or obligation to force life to resume. And one cannot find one's self in that situation without giving thought to the other possibility — that life itself might very well, some January, finding itself being neglected, choose to make a cold the ignominious pretext for its own departure. How messy, undistinguished, and uncomfortable to have, under the sniffles and coughs and the dull, drugged feeling, the lungs creeping full or the heart tripping over itself. How drably uneventful to die of a cold. But it seems, year after year, as if January has established itself as the month for illness, pressing its cold, house-bound days down on human beings trying to draw themselves up toward the sun, prying, as it pries among the buds and shoots of the plant world, for the weaknesses its own touch may convert into fatalities for which and for whom there will be no spring. January, whatever the statistics may be, seems the executioner month. When death comes in some other season of the year, it makes it seem like January.

SPOCRP
(Society for the Prevention of Cruelty to Retired Persons)

Thursday, Jan. 11. For many years the cat population on this place has been regulated by the cruel deus ex machina of the automobiles passing by, those that go by fast and never, or seldom, slow down, and those that come by very slow and leave fast. About three weeks ago the driver of one of the fast ones did slow down and stop and come to the door to tell us he had had an accident involving a black cat which he thought might belong to us. It did, and it was Angelo, and we thanked him for his thoughtfulness, and had no reason to mention to him, in his sorrowful assumption of what our sentiments would have to be, that Angelo was originally a stray, that he had begun, of late, to display a temper that made it unsafe to get near his fangs or claws, and that his departure would, at least, make one less cat mouth to feed on our retirement scale of income. As for the motorists who slow down and then leave fast, we never see them because they always wait until dusk, and the only way we discover the purpose of their slowing down comes the next morning, when there is a stranger cat at our kitchen door. This was probably the way Angelo arrived, so that one could say that what the automobile brings, the automobile sometimes takes away. It happened to Angelo three weeks ago. This morning his replacement was at the door, a veritable feline freak of streetcorner breeding which had come out something that might be called a calico Angora, unbelievably bushily ugly to everybody except SJ, whose unswerving reverence for life, no matter what the superficial appearance, makes her, probably quite without her own knowledge, the best Christian in this family. Like all the stray cats we get, this one had had, up to the very moment of cruel discard, lots of family affection, so that it tried to rub against your leg, and gave you unfrightened cuddling looks and purrings. But it would mean six cat mouths to feed again, when we had already realized that spending nearly two dollars a week for cat food was over a hundred dollars a year and more than any sensible retired couple could afford. Now the first test is whether we name this new monstrosity. If we give it a name, it will stay and be accorded a place in the family. If we continue to snub it, and try to frighten it away from the evening meal, and encourage our own cats to snarl at it, then it might decide to look elsewhere for a home. It is not a very nice thing to drop an unwanted pet on anybody's lawn, especially the lawn of retired persons.

The Woodpile

Friday, Jan. 12. In those growing-up years, on the farm in Newtown, the woodpile was the number one symbol of security. Those who were too young to be aware of the systems of supply for food, or money, or clothing were never in any doubt about the necessity for wood. There had to be sticks in the woodbox in back of the kitchen stove, and in the woodshed, dry and ready to bring into the house. There had to be logs outside the woodshed, ready to be sawed and split. There had to be trees in the woodlot, to be cut down and punged through the snow. Otherwise there was no life. I had a long and thorough schooling in the importance of the woodpile. Yet the other night, when a touch of emergency turned this house primitive, the woodpile flunked the test. The transformer on the utility pole in front of the house had blown with a bright flash and loud report; the weather was below twenty and forecasted for down to zero; the house was full of pipes likely to freeze unless somebody, with an eye on the dwindling pressure in the well-water-system tank, kept rationing drips from one faucet and another. Only a strong fire in the living room fireplace would make it possible for us to stay in the house through the night to keep saving the pipes from disaster. Yet the side porch held only a few small sticks. The only available big chunks lay, snow-encrusted, across the lawn and across the brook, rather far out in the cold night for pensioner blood and heart and muscle and will to tackle. Fortunately, about the moment this drama was to begin, the power came back on. If, when this cold relents, I am ever going to put one thing in shape around here, it has to be that woodpile. A man's woodpile, they used to say, tells all there is to tell about him. I am afraid that still goes.

The Bluefish

Saturday, Jan. 13. It swam, a little snapper, in and out of the harbors of Long Island Sound. It went out to sea and then, carnivorous and fiercely hungry in its young adulthood, came back toward Block Island. One day last September it grabbed the wrong piece of flesh and wound up in a freezer. It journeyed from a freezer on Block Island to one in New Canaan. Today it completed the journey up from New Canaan to this place. In a few days it will be stuffed and baked and gorged upon by this perpetually fish-hungry appetite. The bluefish from Block Island is now almost an annual affair, and a gastronomic event of great delight. The mere thought of it warms me and makes me feel good all over. But the truth is, of course, that no fish is that good. The thing about this fish is its bringer, FR. He has a nice way, from his career rather paralleling mine, of making it clear that he has me, the elder practitioner, on a bit of a pedestal. But that, although it does not hurt, obviously, is not the key to the pleasure that rises between us when we are together. I always have the feeling that he is warm and honest, and that he makes me feel warm and honest toward him, and that this would happen even if there was not this touch of flattery, of homage to an older craftsman, in his attitude. In short, his flattery is the more precious because his whole character, as it comes toward me, convinces me that it is genuine and instinctive, and not with purpose — not even subconscious, sly, unadmitted purpose. We are different in some of the things we believe in and in the slants we take, so that there could be many things between us. Yet there is nothing that separates us except distance. We are friends, and an annual bluefish seals it.

Be Kind to Your Ego

Sunday, Jan. 14. Four months' experience is no eminence from which to deliver advice. But one early conclusion not likely to be changed is that the pensioner should be reasonably kind to his own ego. This is not a recommendation for conceit. It involves, on a more practical level, the functional assurance that keeps an individual moving from one performance to another. The assurance he needs for this is the feeling that he is not doing too badly, that what he is attempting is not too far beyond his capability, and that he is not, by making the effort, risking more than he can afford in the matter of reputation, and most important of all, self-esteem — his reputation with himself. The ego is like the starter on the motor, the gyroscope at

271

sea. The pensioner wants to be careful with it and kind to it to keep it in working order, because without it nothing else is likely to work. Here are a few rules on how he should be kind to his ego:

1. Keep his goals relatively limited and reasonable.

2. Always have more than one goal in view at any particular time, so that there will always be some effort in progress whenever any other effort comes to a halt, either from victory or failure.

3. Avoid last chances. Never trap himself in a situation where he has to make a move that may mean all or nothing.

4. Don't ever, if he finds himself in need of reassurance, go and study himself in a mirror.

The Castle-Home

Monday, Jan. 15. This old house could tell us a thing or two about living. It remembers things we have begun to forget, about how we ourselves once behaved in it. It might taunt us out of our retirement syndrome tendency, which began even before actual retirement, to regard any entrance by the outside world into the castle-home as an unsettling intrusion, to be guarded against and prevented, if possible, to be suffered stoically and terminated early if it cannot be prevented. This crotchety instinct not to be disturbed in one's house is a hardening of the amenities which afflicts some of us as we grow old. It often becomes stronger than that sense of loneliness which is more commonly recognized as a problem for senior citizens. We cannot recreate, even if we remember it, the pride and joy we took in sharing this same home in the years when we were making it. We forget that the real way to feel secure in the possession of a castle is to run it as an open house. We give ourselves the alibi that we no longer have the energy and strength to cope with that kind of life. But we often use up much more vital resource worrying about how to escape from it, or deal with it when it proves inescapable, than we would to move cheerfully into it. The old house knows; it is still lively, if we listen intently, with the sound of voices in all its rooms; still warm with close encounters; still too big and handsome ever to be allowed to stay empty for long. But the real point of view is not that of the house, but our own. It takes ceaseless sharing to make one's home truly one's own. To make the castle secure, lower the drawbridge.

"Just Settin' "

Tuesday, Jan. 16. It was not a lapse in language or in diction if, in your memories, some family oldster responded to an inquiry as to what he or she was doing by saying, "Just settin'." It was not a corruption of the verb *to sit,* although sitting was obviously part of what the oldster was doing. It was, instead, a borrowing from the verb *to set,* as in to set eggs for hatching under a brooding hen, which then became a setting hen. "Just settin' " means sitting in the same place for a long time in a resigned, brooding mood, waiting patiently in case something hatches. This was what I did for an hour and a half this afternoon, the sun on this amazing January day warming things up toward fifty degrees, the fading symptoms of my cold leaving me without energy, and Barkis contentedly exercising herself around the frozen pond, so that I sat there, on a low brick wall, just settin' for the whole time. No particular piece of brooding disturbed the peaceful vacancy of mind I was experiencing. No idea or perception hatched itself underneath my haunches. It might as well have been time excerpted from experience and from the record except that, now and then, I would lean back, thrust my lungs forward, and take in a little more breath. This occasional deeper breath became the only semblance of exercise in the afternoon. It seemed, each time, arduous enough. Nonetheless, this session of just settin' was part of preparation and conditioning for some future hatching out of greater action and more vigor. It was a whole world removed from ''just sittin'.'' The ''i'' word is, quite possibly, a surrender. The ''e'' word is a stubborn act of continuing life. I stayed there this afternoon until the rays of the sun came level and the chill in the ground and from the pond began to creep up under them.

Rules for Reminiscing

Wednesday, Jan. 17. It is not true that the garrulous old man wanders farther from the truth than some younger conversationalist would do. He usually puts out as good a mixture of fact and fancy as anybody else who recounts a story or recreates a situation for the benefit of a captive audience. The old man's trouble is that he reminisces too often, into too slight an opening, so that it is the pushy frequency of his tales, not the proportion of unintentional embellishment in them, that turns people off. The first rule for us oldsters when we get to the age of reminiscence is, then, don't. But it is not an absolute don't. We should carry ourselves ready to respond to any quiet request for our memory of how things seemed in other days. But we should never, never, never volunteer an "I remember when" or "When I first went to work" or any of those thousand openings so dear to us because they seem to infiltrate us right back into that stream of life which has begun to swirl on past us. Rule number two covers the kind of reminiscing we should produce in the event we are asked. Never begin with a speculative-sounding "Now let me see." Train yourself to go directly to one concrete and briefly phrased response presented without embroidery and so shaped that, unless somebody persists in asking another question or imploring amplification, what you say in this first response will wrap the reminiscence up and leave the conversation free to veer where everybody else may please. "The answer to your question, sir, is that in 1922 girls' basketball was an extremely popular sport played in middy blouses and bloomers." Soon you will begin to gain a reputation that will be dear to your ego — that you are not like other oldsters, not at all.

Reactivating the Corpuscle

Thursday, Jan. 18. In the glory of youth an illness is an imprisonment from which the human metabolism itself rebounds, voluntarily and eagerly, the moment the virus lets go. After a certain stage in life has been reached — this present stage — each illness is an episode in which one dies a little bit, giving up ground and vigor that do not recover themselves automatically the moment the actual symptoms have disappeared. Today this Vitamin C version of cold packed up its annoyances and left. I went to bed last night without any coughing spell and slept through without any middle-of-the-night lozenge or aspirin. I was, therefore, not only feeling better but ready to begin escalating activity. It is at this kind of moment that the pensioner discovers that

279

neither mind nor body is eager to leap out of the complacent nothingness of effort which was excused and enforced by the illness and recommended by every friend and relative. One does not, after all, necessarily fret to be doing something. One doesn't automatically rush back toward normal routines of exertion and accomplishment. One could, quite easily, be content to let the world stay shrunk and throttled down to the area and speed to which it had been confined by the weakness one has just escaped. This, if one tolerated it, would soon prove a brand of therapeutic suicide. If one is going to live, and not die by ignominious degrees of minor afflictions, like a cold, or a week of arthritis, one must address that red corpuscle in strict military terms, order it back into uniform and into circulation and out on patrol. Dutifully, today, in the afternoon, I compelled myself into the chore of slipping on overalls and warm work coat and sallied forth, stopping at the garage for a pair of pruners so that I would be armed if I should feel up to skirmishing with some bush along my path. It was a short patrol, with only a few desultory passes at the enemy, but it was at least a small slice of a beginning, not that additional accrual of ending which will be the departing gift of every small sickness at our age, if we let it be. One, two, three, hup! Get going out there, you little red b———!

Routines

Friday, Jan. 19. This morning JL at the radio station called up and changed our weekly taping session from afternoon to morning and I was annoyed because, obviously, I had expected to go on taping at two o'clock every Friday afternoon for the rest of my life. I have also been annoyed, all week, with the mailman, because he has changed his hours, coming at 10:15 when I, obviously, expected him to continue coming at 11:15 for the rest of both our lives. But there is something mixed in with my annoyance. Perhaps the outside world does me a favor when, with its rude, arbitrary, and seemingly thoughtless changes that happen to affect my own routines, it mixes things up for me, changing fixed patterns which might have been becoming too fixed. I may be feeling, inside myself, a slight freshening of enterprise, a re-mix of all my psychological conditioning for function in this world, all because some outside agency has upset my assembly-line schedule. Perhaps it was time I had a different pattern of Friday. Perhaps it does make for better mornings if the mailman keeps me guessing. Perhaps the real time to worry comes when one's routines are so self-contained and self-generated and self-perpetuating and so independent of the rest of the world that no outside force could alter the mix. There has to be a Golden Age mean somewhere between the routine that can help provide form and structure and security for life and the routine that threatens to turn itself into an atrophying straitjacket.

Inaugural: Era of Non-Feeling?

Saturday, Jan. 20. I wish I had a job. I wish I had an absolute necessity to face today's events and face myself and resolve, to my own momentary satisfaction, at least, just what I make of this Richard Nixon. Never in human history, I would judge, has any individual in a position of leadership had the citizens of his own nation in such a permanently helpless state of confusion as to their own real feelings about him. It has been possible to hate him and to vote for him, to support him and hope for his failure. Some of us have been able to rate every public attitude of his as something spurious and false yet cast our lot with him because we recoil from what might conceivably be involved in trying to live with a touch of the genuine in somebody else. The horrible, frightening, fending-off thing about him is that there is no way for us, his fellow citizens, to extend compassion toward him, to feel sorry for him in his situation, in his life with himself, to sympathize with him, to imagine sharing his burden with him, to break through to the humanity in him. It is as if his whole life had been designed, even after that one indisputably human and revealing moment when he told us we wouldn't have him to kick around any more, for making sure that it had a kind of movement and propulsion that would never be exposed to kicking around — or to kindness and gentleness, either. Some thing, some it, was inaugurated in Washington today. Late tonight it simulated a dancer, laughing in the arms of a warm and aventurous-looking blonde. If only it could learn to do something as if it were not watching itself and pacing itself every second of the way! But I am not only concerned, here, with what may be the deficiencies of Mr. Nixon. What also upsets me is my own inability, even at the end of a lifetime of public observation and uninhibited analysis of people, to come up with any words which can really explain Richard Nixon to me, or to a couple hundred million other Americans, or tell any of us what we really think of him. That mass paralysis of conclusion about him creates a strange, nerveless kind of existence for the whole country. We all want to *feel* something again.

Let Others Look Their Age

Sunday, Jan. 21. Never study yourself in a mirror, we said the other day in compiling rules for a successful pampering of the aging ego. Keep to those casual glances necessary for shaving or straightening a tie. For purposes of noting your own general appearance, develop a sideways flash-look technique, as if your vision were limited to the flick of the shutter on a camera. The reason for such warnings is this: There lies, hidden in the depths of the glass, a story you need never confront so long as you do keep your glances casual and oblique. It is one of nature's indulgences to each of us that it is by no means necessary that we ever see ourselves precisely as others do. Just how we achieve the miracle of seeing gray hair, wrinkles, sagging chins, drooping, loosening throats, protruding veins and the first slight stoop-posture in all our contemporaries without ever suspecting that the same concessions to an equal number of years may be present in our own appearance — how we achieve this miracle is in itself a mystery, but not one to be quarreled with, or risked in needlessly excessive scrutinizing encounters with some stray idiot piece of glass that has been backed up against a wall.

January Thaw

Monday, Jan. 22. This January is turning out to be an act of mercy. There has been no ice or snow, nothing to shovel, nothing to worry about when driving. Temperatures steadily above normal, day after day, allay fears of fuel shortages and balance off the over-consumption commandeered by the cold autumn. This is good for pocketbooks old and young. More than that, this kind of January offers a daily psychological reprieve for the spirit. This would be the month when severe weather, if it came, would have its best chance of hanging on until it posed a test of wills, a struggle of survival itself, to human beings in their clothes, their automobiles, their offices, their homes. Because it is placed by this kind of threat January is always, no matter what kind of weather it actually delivers, the longest month of the year. This January, although pleasant, has already lasted forever, and still there is no evening or morning without the thought that Messrs. Zero and Snow may be about to take possession of the season to which they hold title. But they, in a monotonous spell of charity, stay away, and peddle their challenges and discomforts north and south and west of us, but not here. If I belonged to a group of senior citizens I would propose a resolution of praise and gratitude to this January for taking it easy on us. Unaffiliated, I sat down by the pond this afternoon watching juncos flitter close to the open water at the inlet end.

The Harvest Years

Tuesday, Jan. 23. While this diarist is struggling with the problem of how to adjust himself to life at sixty-five, Lyndon Johnson is dead at sixty-four. He was four years out of the Presidency. Richard Nixon, the other day, celebrated his sixtieth birthday, and has just begun serving four more years in the Presidency. The age at which I am concerned with the problems of staying alive and functioning with some decent degree of purpose and grace is, then, very close to the age zone within which this nation finds its leadership. By its choices it shows that it considers men in the neighborhood of sixty best equipped, properly matured and, at the same time, adequately vigorous for the toughest and most important job in the world. Quite incongruously our system, which doesn't like to trust men with top responsibility until they are near the sixty mark, proceeds to put the retirement stigma on ordinary people almost immediately thereafter. There is this relatively narrow zone of years in which the human being is considered in best shape and condition for exhibition and testing in the great fair of public events. When we get ready to use men in their highest capacities in the highest places we already trespass upon, but perhaps also arrest, their own time of natural disintegration and decay. The harvest years for the nation's most special human crop, that developed for top leadership, are the very same years when the rest of us have already begun to slow down. Maybe the best of all formulas for life at sixty-five would be this: Get elected president of something.

Man and Tree

Wednesday, Jan. 24. A man can tell the age of a tree by counting its rings after he has cut it down. A tree will also measure the age of the man who cuts it down. After, late this afternoon, the tree in question had slowly slipped toward the ground, I audited the combination of saw, get-your-breath, stand-up-and-survey and play-with-Barkis time that had gone into the exploit. I spent two hours today and an hour and a half yesterday on a tree no more than thirty feet tall and eleven inches in diameter. The same amount of cut, if undertaken by the young farm boy I once used to know and be, would have taken about ten minutes. To audit the reasons it is now so different is to indulge in an extended lamentation for the days of such youth. Sawing a tree off close to the ground requires operating on one's knees. The mere getting down and getting up now requires a thoughtful effort compared to the automatic, unconscious movement of half a century ago Operating a saw in such a position has now become an awkwardness where once the young body could supple itself into it with some grace. The number of strokes one can take with a saw in such a position is now strictly limited to something around thirty or forty for a relatively good persistence as compared to uninterrupted production of the three hundred strokes needed for a fall in the days when young muscle might have been boasting to elderly supervision about its own limitless endurance. The very process of gulping down nature's free air has developed complications. The oldster seems to have forgotten how to breathe while engaged in concentrated physical effort; the youngster never did anything but open up, unconsciously, for as much air as he needed. In spite of all these differences, one thing in the relationship between a man and a tree remains the same whatever the respective ages involved. Once the struggle has been joined, it has to be to the death. The tree has to come down, even though there may be a danger the man will come down too, or first. Any time you see a man and a tree facing one another, know that the struggle is mortal.

The War-Peace Twilight

Thursday, Jan. 25. One of the minor comforts of old age ought to be that one has attained opinions and judgments and definitions to which one can hold with some degree of certainty. I was a little boy growing up during World War I and, immediately after, an automatic part of the national ritual of homage to victory and its generals. I evangelized (journalistically) the coming of World War II but escaped service in it. I welcomed the Korean "police action" as the first sample of actual enforcement of the world's law against war. Because the war in Vietnam was a violation rather than an enforcement of that same law I opposed it from the start, and I ought, therefore, to be cheerful in this, the week in which that war is supposedly ending. But the feeling I have been living with in this week of transition from war to peace is the feeling that there is no appreciable difference between them, that both their content and our behavior in them have somehow now become the same thing. It is as if civilization, after pretending and hoping for so long to be a struggle between light and darkness, between good and evil, between morality and amorality, has finally abandoned itself to a perpetual and henceforth irremediable twilight in which damnation and salvation each share equal portions of the other. It seems to make no difference in this twilight what values we say we exalt or what goals we claim we are seeking; the inner essences remain the same and we arrive, again and again, at the same ultimate taste in the mouth. At first we thought it clever semantic strategy that the Communists began using the word peace when they meant war, as if they were trying to trick us. Now it seems possible they were just a little ahead of us in bowing to the Kafkaesque perception which has become the only kind of truth in an era and a world where truth itself is no longer any certainty but a denial of all certainties. Having believed for the last twenty-five years of my life that war represented the greatest horror and idiocy of which mankind is capable, I now come to the suspicion that what we call peace is merely a superficially different code of behavior serving the same principles in search of the same ends and imposing cruelties no less barbaric merely because they display less obvious spill of blood and gore. If there is a human problem, and a cure for it, it must lie far beyond such sophomoric themes as peace and war, good and evil, civilized and uncivilized, and beyond such choice of weapons — words versus swords, bullets versus ballots — which our intent makes equally inhumane. And unless such uneasy speculation can be called some degree of it, understanding is something I am not going to be able to snuggle down with toward the end of this journey.

Luncheon at Essex

Friday, Jan. 26. For any attempted journey to understanding, substitute a drive down to Essex. This is the kind of day we oldsters do well. We move in our own time zone, exempted from the urgency of getting some place or getting home by any certain hour. We operate in a congenial concept of minimal mission; we are going to Essex; we need not do anything more than go there; if, on the way, or while there, or on the way home, we feel like adding some peripheral activity, that is still an even-paced, unhurried, non-compressed low priority. Today I walked down to the docks and sat there, in a moment of loneliness and quiet, watching a mallard make love to his mate, until people arrived and began throwing bread on the waters. Meanwhile

C walked in the other direction and looked in at the bookstore. We exchanged our modest observations and drove home by the river roads along that stretch of the lower Connecticut which is, by some miracle, the longest unspoiled riverbank mileage in all America. Not until we were almost home did we begin talking about what we then realized had been the most pleasurable experience of the day, the few moments we had spent looking down at a particularly neat and lovely knot garden in the side yard of one of the handsome houses on Main Street in Essex. The idea of a knot garden turned out to be the thing we had brought home with us; should we start now slipping and breeding for it, from our own big box bush, it would probably take more years than we have left. Nonetheless we might begin. A quiet drive, on either side of a luncheon in Essex, can happen upon such an idea and nourish such new initiatives for old hands and backs. But we do not have to unless we want to. We are quiet, elderly pilgrims, modestly luxuriating in a combination of involvement and freedom, making our way gently through scenes we have seen and yet not seen before. Never feel sorry for us when, among the busy, purposeful travelers of this world, you notice our seemingly inconsequential presence on the road.

The Shrewd Indulgence

Saturday, Jan. 27. Yesterday we drove down to Essex and had lunch at what we often feel to be the finest place for food in Connecticut — the old Griswold Inn, now under a new management that seems intelligently intent on retaining, with some pleasing small improvements, the best of the old. The luncheon cost eleven dollars, including two gin-and-tonics. It was excellent food, all we could eat, along with the pleasant change of eating out in the finest style. We could have had lunch at some pie-and-sandwich place for $5.50.

But this was a good bargain because we were satisfying ourselves with the best at a cost which, although it may have been twice that of a pie-and-sandwich place, was also only half what it would have cost us to have a good dinner out. By sacrificing only the time of day involved, by making it lunch instead of dinner, we had luxury at only half the price. Some other noon we may be in a casual mood for economizing and we will eat accordingly. But one of the steadfast pleasures of life is that of feeling luxurious, of indulging ourselves in something that has distinction. And the simple point is that, especially for people who are masters of their own time, the extravagance can still be enjoyed at half price. You could go to the same restaurant in the evening and buy approximately the same amount of food and service, and cost yourself twenty-two dollars. Six hours earlier we went first class, in spite of our lower fixed-income status. Good retirement planning, good retirement economy, makes room, when the mood strikes, for such selective and shrewd indulgence.

The Twenty-Seven-Minute Tree

Sunday, Jan. 28. Oh, for the body of one's youth! That was the lamentation here after two afternoons had been spent torturing down a dying elm which, in the days of that youth, would have been a twenty-minute exploit at the most. Yesterday afternoon, sawing off the smaller branches and then cutting the main trunk into short lengths, I worked better but still finished exhausted. Today, after C had carried away the brush and the smaller branches, I disposed of the larger pieces. Then I did something I had not intended to do again this winter, not after the encounter in which a mere eleven-inch diameter had proved such a difficult giant for me. I went over and looked at the next dead elm, another eleven-incher. I sank to my knees, began working the saw peacefully and easily, and found it easing its way swiftly through the wood. I still grew tired of arm and short of breath, but in a very few minutes the blade had reached a point where I thought Barkis had better be on her chain so she would not be frolicking near the tree if it fell. I returned, sawed a little more, stood up, pushed the trunk, found it wavering, gave it a triumphant final pressure, and down it went. Total elapsed time, twenty-seven minutes. For this visit back to the illusion of youth, two things were responsible. One was almost automatic — practice helps, in the business of sawing. Make a routine, and sooner or later you lapse into it. The other thing responsible for the twenty-seven-minute tree was something C said the other day, suggesting that we tend to get psychologically older than our muscles and backs really are. Out there this afternoon I was not testing age, or pressing toward a time record, or being old, or being young. I was just so much flesh and sinew with a tool, not doing a single thing other than sawing. Before that kind of approach the tree surrendered.

It Never Happens to Us

Monday, Jan. 29. 1. Everybody around us may die, but we don't. Everyone else grows old, but not us. In battle, everyone is killed but us. Death on the highways claims anybody and everybody, but we escape. Whatever happens as routine and inevitable to the rest of mankind — of that we ourselves are always spared. In our theater, we stage our favorite tragedies as a formal reaffirmation to ourselves of such exemption. Our therapeutic catharsis experience is gained from our own immune, antiseptic, uninvolved (except insofar as we choose to pretend to be involved) dip into the trouble that is happening to somebody else.

2. What we think of as the passing of time exists only in the physical world. In the mind, which is where we live by and with ourselves and our own concepts of ourselves, time stands still or there is no time. The past, the present, and the future do not move in rotation, or in sequence, or in any general concerted progress. In a physical minute it is possible to encompass a lifetime in the mind. We give time the attributes it has, we invent it, but we cannot feel it, or make ourselves co-travelers in the journeys we imagine it to be making.

These are two thoughts C set down, the other day, after I asked her why we do not detect in ourselves the aging process so obvious in other people.

The Pipe and the Chair

Tuesday, Jan. 30. Pipes in the cellar and chairs in the parlor that may wear out before we do — they are the key threat to our effort to live out these final years in something like the modest style and comfort to which we have become accustomed. I kept in touch with the retirement experience of the bright, gentle couple who were our predecessors in this town. When he left the job I was taking, he had provided himself with a retirement cottage on a riverbank down in the New London territory where he had lived when he was, for a time, city editor over a young reporter named Eugene O'Neill. His riverbank home served his purpose well and lasted him his lifetime. But his widow was soon forced to sell the place, and what forced her to sell was the failure of a water pump she could not afford to spend part of her small capital to replace. If the water pump, a matter of a few hundred dollars, had not happened to fail, she might have lived on in their house and so escaped becoming a renter of small and smaller rooms for the rest of her life. Here, in this house, the water pump failed a year ago, and we thought it was lucky for us it failed then when we could still pay for the new one out of a weekly wage. But the plumbing account is one that can never be closed. Our new tank system maintains a higher pressure than the old. Last week one of the water pipes we ourselves had installed when we moved in thirty-one years ago suddenly yielded to the higher pressure and began spraying the cellar. The plumbers came and replaced a long section of pipe in not much more than an hour, which was good news. But there are other pipes of the same vintage under the same pressure. We read, the other day, of a pensioner who had resolved to spend his new spare time going to a trade school so he could learn to do his own plumbing. It is a marvelous idea, but we doubt that he ever does it, and we know I won't. We are not going to be able to continue living in this house if it depends on my becoming a handyman. It is going to depend, so far as plumbing is concerned, on how long we live and how lucky we are with our pipes. And that leaves the problem of the chair for tomorrow's entry.

The Chair, Etc.

Wednesday, Jan. 31. New twelve years ago, the damask-covered Chippendale-style wing chair has the place of honor in the parlor, at the right side of the fireplace. Occasionally, in winter twilights, C sits there to read. But the only regular use for it has been on those rare evenings when we entertain, and on Christmas morning, when I sit in it as the presents are opened. Nonetheless, in spite of such sparing use, the chair has begun to show its undercloth through the damask. The odds are that just as I am not going to become a handyman with the plumbing, so we are not going to become upholsterers. We are going to try to continue hiring this sort of thing done. The upholsterer, if we hire him, will probably charge us $180 for putting new damask on this $250 chair. Our danger is that we may think of this as a single matter and figure out how we can afford it, and go ahead with it, without bothering to calculate that, like plumbing, furniture and furnishings are not guaranteed to have the grace to last as long as their owners shall live. There are other chairs in line, and we know which they are when we want to admit it to ourselves, and there is paint getting to be obscenely dirty, and there are drapes which, when they begin to crumble from the sun they have taken, will cost like Versailles — and the realistic truth about all this is that no, we cannot have it, not out of what we have or what we are making now. The longer we drift making piecemeal expenditures on a scale we cannot possibly afford, the more rude and perhaps desperate the final reckoning may be. Of course it may be these "things" which, after all, outlast us and thus spare us the expense. The damask may go from our cheeks, the obscene crumbling may take place inside our own fabric, before we go broke. We have to try to hit the right mixture of common sense and deliberate gamble in an unending series of dreary, disheartened decisions. Or — what really seems much more sensible — perhaps we should do what Will Rogers said we Americans do so well — go broke in a Cadillac — and do the whole place over one more time and let the consequences catch us if they can.

Forsythia

Thursday, Feb. 1. No worry over the economic adjustments the pensioner must face — no recognition of the choices that may have to be made between the expensive reupholstering of a chair and some shabby stratagem — should be allowed to obscure the fact that there are some luxuries which are free. One of these — pure gold — is standing right now, on this first day of February, on the chest of drawers in the front hall, lighting the hall, reflecting itself in the mirror behind it, giving a sense of well-being and prosperity to the whole establishment. It represents, first, a cutting of branches from one of the front line of shrubs that makes and turns our corner. It represents, second, the no-cost process of forcing, by which branches clipped in winter and placed in water in the house proceed to imitate the spring to come. It represents, third, the always excellent and sometimes hush-inspiring talent C has for arranging things in bloom. For the life and beauty this brings into the house, for what it does to the heart and soul on the first day of February, and for the fresh new creation it spreads out from its own standing place over every possible minor shabbiness the caretaker mind can certify to be lurking all through this old house, waiting to pounce on straitened, pensioner circumstances, this managed burst of forsythia carries the worth of a million dollars.

The Nothing Day

Friday, Feb. 2. Nothing that I shall set down reflects on any of the other participants in this particular day. There was nothing different or lacking in the way C made breakfast. In the *Times* it was not Reston's fault that this morning's assault on Nixon seemed boring. The young man with whom I taped three broadcasts was courteous and helpful as usual. The good friend with whom I lunched and the other friends I encountered had not suddenly shrunk in their ability to be good company. It was not that I was any less happy than usual to have SJ coming home for the weekend from the big city. No, nothing in this day was the fault of the outside world or of any other person in it. It was all me. I thought nothing, perceived nothing, gave nothing, took nothing, felt nothing, wanted nothing and asked nothing, and, except for the barest minimum in compulsory chores, did nothing from the moment I got up until the early time I went to bed. Even this entry is being written the next day. What makes such a day? What can take a man and put him in the midst of people and things and strip him of any inclination to acknowledge them or participate in any kind or degree of relationship with them? All I like to think is that, in a more primitive state of civilization, if a caveman succumbed to a nothing day, he accepted it as a natural, perhaps sensible experience and, when he returned to a capacity to feel something, never dreamed of letting guilt over a wasted day be one of those feelings.

Once More, a Newsman
Saved the World

Saturday, Feb. 3. Every newspaperman fancies himself a potential maker of history as well as a reporter and commentator. The possibility I am about to weave is as good a sample of such conceit as any, and perhaps has as much truth as any. Its suppositions tie in neatly together; the two men who might denouce them are now both dead and it is not likely that the kind of easy and informal influence that might have been involved would be included in any memoranda or diaries that may have survived. This, at any rate, is the way this one went. Prescott Bush, having received the Republican nomination to run for the Unites States Senate in 1952, made a point of having lunch with me and asked me to suggest campaign issues. I was precise and passionate that the only major issue of our time was that of a world of law. The subsequent Bush career, both in his campaigning to Connecticut voters and on the national scene, was full of speeches on the world law theme, unnatural as that sometimes seemed coming from a Republican conservative, a Wall Street broker-golfer. Senator Bush also became a frequent golfing companion for President Eisenhower. In fact, they played together at Burning Tree during the Suez crisis of 1956, the crisis which terminated after Eisenhower, in support of peace-restoring votes and actions at the United Nations, proclaimed that, if we were ever to have a world of law, it must be law which applied to our friends — in that instance England, France, and Israel, who had launched their attack on Nasser Egypt — as well as to those who were not our friends. Does the chain of influence now appear quite clear? Yours truly to Bush and Bush, four years later, to Eisenhower who, by his pronouncement to the world, took the United Nations to the great temporary peak of its power and prestige . . . ? No one can prove it or disprove it. No one can take away, either, the slight chance that there may have been a slight chain of influence involved. And although newspapermen are supposed to be great cynics, they are also notorious for being able to make do, where their own egos are concerned, with just such slight establishments of their own importance in the history of their time.

A Clue, if There Should Be No Other

Sunday, Feb. 4. I set it down, for the record, that about Tuesday of last week I developed a feeling of soreness and strain in the left shoulder region extending over and down into the top left portion of the chest. By Thursday I was also feeling a slight case of stomach upset which, by Friday, had translated itself into what seemed to be an upward pressure in the diaphragm. For a day I avoided all physical exertion. Yesterday, impatient with such a stalemate, I deliberately went out and sawed wood. I then ate heavily and went through the evening and to bed feeling quite as usual again. Today, finishing the large limb I had begun sawing yesterday, I received, from my alarmist nerves, occasional bulletins of slight pains in the chest again. I paused and rested frequently, as I do all the time these days. And that is that. The medical column in this morning's newspaper was headlined "Chest Pains Often Clue to Heart Trouble." But I never do read any column with a heading like that, and I did not read it today. I will not be likely to consult anybody, or seek any update in that daily little white pill I have been taking, or do anything more than be a little more nervous and take it a little bit easier when I get myself involved in some match with a log stronger than I am. Meanwhile, however, this is down for the record. A clue, if there should be no other.

Manchester

Monday, Feb. 5. Manchester, incorporated in 1823 as a split-off from East Hartford, got to be a town later than the majority of its fellow Connecticut communities, and now it has ceased being a town, in everything except label, ahead of many others. Neither a town nor a city, it illustrates the de-characterizing influences and deficiencies of that bastard brand of American life called suburbia. Once suburbia sets in, the victim town finds itself continually betrayed by a majority of its own citizens who head blindly into the formless new and who accept, at least until it is much too late to reverse anything, the idea that growth is in itself an all in all. The loss of form, distinction and unity lead to an abandonment of character until, sooner or

316

later, the word Manchester, which once summoned up an economic, social and political entity, is drained dry of all except the most superficial connotations. Manchester is the place which lies off super-highway exits 93 through 95. There are, of course, different evaluations of what Manchester and Manchester life were like when they were something more than food, fuel and residence at the end of super-highway exits. It was, in objective actuality, a mill town much more beautiful and attractive than all other New England mill towns because it flowered and grew under the benevolent paternalism of an unusual mill-owning family, the Cheneys, one of whom, back in the founding past, was an artist who sold enough paintings to provide the capital his brothers used to open their first mill. When, a century later, nylon knifed silk and the Depression and cheaper Southern labor ruined the New England mills, the benevolent paternalism of the Cheneys dwindled wistfully to an end, and the town itself then proceeded to expand, witlessly, tastelessly, into a drab destiny of providing bedrooms and shopping centers for people who earned their living elsewhere. Only the town lines on the various roads leading in establish or assert any differences between this piece of suburbia and all the rest of the widening no-roots land which is currently putting ever greater distance between the two precariously surviving meaningfulnesses of city and country. I say I am from Manchester, when asked, as if it were statistical information, not a matter for chauvinist satisfaction or pride. Once it was a locus to fight for, and glory in, and try to preserve and improve, to love and to cherish. Then I gave it my heart, and it gave heart back to me. There was a town, and there was an editor, and they had their moments. I hope its present-day thinkers and doers will forgive me if I confess I liked it better when.

The Bitch Log and the Sixteen-Pound Sledge

Tuesday, Feb. 6. The exuberances and prides and vigors of youth exhume themselves, like jealous ghosts, to come and mock their own comeuppances in old age. My memory of logs and sledges begins with the day a farmer neighbor considered me old enough to be admitted to the world of men and, seeing me about to split a log in the woods, reversed my approach and tingled my college freshman virginal senses by saying, "No, boy. You split a woman from the butt end. You split a log from the tit end." I have never, in the succeeding years, some twenty of them spent away from logs of any kind, had any difficulty remembering that the way to get the log itself playing along with your efforts is to start the

319

wedges in the smaller end. Today, tackling the big branch from the front yard maple, my trouble was not one of technique but one of muscle. In the last summer vacation of the college years, working on the rough landscaping of a new estate, I worked eight-hour days swinging a sixteen-pound sledge on rock, breaking it for stone walls and road beds. I had slim arms with inner ripples like those in a tiger's shoulder. I had a good, smart back, and I had rhythm. Sixteen years later, when I needed to provide myself with a sledge for this farm, the proud memory of those rock-breaking eight-hour days dictated the selection of another sixteen-pounder. That was the tool I was trying to use today on a maple log that, even when approached from the right end, was behaving, if I may lapse into an imagined continuation of man-to-man conversation with my neighbor, like a tight bitch. The sledge hammer arm-scaled forty pounds just to carry out there, and at the end of the day, with not all the necessary splitting yet done, it weighed a hundred pounds a swing.

Avernus

Wednesday, Feb. 7. You'd think one of the blessings of maturity would be the privilege of knowing, at last, what you really think about some of the issues mankind is always debating. But the more I withdraw from that incessant involvement which never left time to think — the more I do try to think — the less firm and the more shaken I become. I staked a whole lifetime of occupational effort on such propositions as the improvability of man, or the futility and basic weakness of the use of force. I had, through all those working years, a mystical dedication to the idealistic side of such questions which was strong enough and blind enough and insistent enough to succeed in blotting out, or rationalizing away, all the contrary evidence which kept pushing its troublesome ugliness into the human picture. Now I find myself in retreat, perhaps heading toward defeat, on all such fronts. I am not sure the nature of man changes at all except for disguise and refinement and therefore possibly increased ultimate amount in the cruelty man employs toward man. I credit more innocence to the caveman using his club than I do to a modern civilization that even builds itself atomic bombs. And at the moment, primarily because it seems that Nixon has just made a cease-fire in Vietnam by a process of "bombing Hanoi back to the negotiating table," and because all the arguments which try to cling, as I would like to cling, to the proposition that it was not force which persuaded Hanoi to resume negotiating seem wistful and weak, I am on the verge of accepting the theory that the bombing did do it. I believe that to accept such a theory, to agree, even for an instant, that the world must run itself on such a basis, is equivalent to agreeing to the permanent damnation of this world, equivalent to the abandonment of all hope. But I also am close to thinking that human nature, if it is really changing in any direction, may be changing for the worse. In that case it cannot make very much difference if I abandon my own fierce emotional insistence that since the end-justifies-the-means use of force is wrong in principle, it can't possibly produce good results. Once I thought I could live only by such faith. Now I am afraid, heart-sick afraid, that I am beginning to find the hard, mocking point of view more comfortable and, if this could be the word, livable. How I hate, at this late stage, to begin trying to live a lie!

One True God

Thursday, Feb. 8. That which I worshipped with mixed wonder and contentment when a boy I worship still in my old age. I sprawled out in it barefoot, or sought it out in the southern doorway of a barn when the ground was covered with blizzard, or climbed college towers to lie in it high above the spring murmur of the campus. I took a stroke from it once in the deceptive dryness of North Africa but did not allow that experience ever to alter my full acceptance of it, at high noon, in a field of hay or on a tennis court. We have been friends forever, even if, reflecting and intensifying itself as if from burnished brass, it dealt death to plants I had raised. In my book it has been incapable of wrong. The yearly optimum of existence comes when I am able to be out in it wearing the absolute minimum in bathing trunks. I spread myself out before it, receptive and grateful, content to go through all of life doing no more than it bids me do. The dark days of my life are the dark days. The longest days of my life, endurance-wise, were back in December, when sun-days were shortest. Then outdoors and whatever pretense of chore I was making closed down at 4:15. Today there was the same comparable amount of light at five o'clock and the day went that much better. It was cold out today, after so many mild days. But if I turned my face into the sun and kept the wind at my back I could feel the growing strength of my returning friend, giver of life and joy, renewer of enterprise, seducer of youth, comforter of age. I would like to be buried in it, by some process in which it would be the only element working on my remains, drying and shriveling them down to dust but keeping them always warm and dry. But first I am beginning to get that feeling (and C was ordering seeds when I came in late this February afternoon) that, with the help of my friend and master, I am going to make it into another spring.

How Do Pensioners
Get New Cars?

Friday, Feb. 9. I didn't tell it here at the time, but on that October day when SJ and I were driving Barkis home there was a side-swipe encounter just this side of Hartford which tore a chrome strip off the right front fender of the Impala. It would cost forty dollars to replace. The other day I noticed that the right front hub cap was missing. The question is whether I invest a little more money in this car, or whether it continues without its normal chrome, without its hub cap, and thus sustains and accepts its first mark of shabbiness. The Impala will, this August, be five years old. But at our pace of car use it has only 35,000 miles on it. There has been no mechanical trouble of any kind since the day we paid for it with one three-thousand-dollar check and drove it home. But now a piece of chrome and a hub cap are gone, and I notice two small, unexplained dark spots on the front seat upholstery, and I leap from this to the question of whether or not we are going to outlive this Impala, and give myself the answer that yes, apparently we are going to survive long enough to be faced with the need of buy at least one more new car. Right away I am able to list some realistic considerations: (1) I am not likely, ever again, to be able to write a check for three thousand dollars, even if that would still buy a car. (2) I would have to be out of my mind to consider using an installment plan. (3) Even more than frayed furniture, the quality and condition of the car a pensioner drives constitutes the face he shows the world. The furniture he can keep in a dim house that has no guests. The car he himself displays everywhere to everybody. (4) Unless, then, my current balancing of the books includes the regular provision of special untouchable amounts which will make possible the writing of a big new check years from now, I am not making it financially, but merely living in a foolish dream world which is going to blow up some fateful day and leave us reduced either to charity or to penury. Or am I merely luxuriating in grim thoughts, expecting that, at the proper moment, a generous customer for "the land" is going to fit the Cinderella slipper to us for the remainder of our lives? But, barring the slipper, how do pensioners ever get new cars? The answer is that I don't know if they do, or, if they do, how. My best guess is that they look for a three-year-old used model in good condition.

Is There Such a Thing as a Second Chance?

Saturday, Feb. 10. It is now more than five months, almost the first half of a year, that I have been in this new state of life. It seems unbelievable that so formidable a chunk of time should have disappeared so swiftly. What is, unfortunately, quite credible, because it is quite plain, is that this period — almost half the time I have allotted myself for experimental progress — has been so low in visible accomplishment and movement forward. I have done some work, but it has not been polishing itself off into any finished product. There has been no instant, miraculous opening of bright new paths. I am beginning to discover that, in terms of getting intentions realized and moving closer to ambitious targets, this life is a lot like the old life. The romantic idea that I was having a second chance, that I was about to be privileged to do part of my life over again, has begun to weaken under the dull gray impact of a suspicion that if I were indeed to have some miraculous chance to make the journey a second time, completely free to do exactly what I really wanted to do, I would then end up doing exactly what I have already done once. Is this pensioner epilogue, then, merely going to be one more chapter in the same old story? Is the fantasy that now I would have time and freedom to create or seize opportunities I never took before wearing itself out? Am

I now squandering time because I have no real vital push to seize and exercise that freedom? Or do I write a new chapter? I still swear I will try. But that laggard part, that inertia, that non-will, that not-great-enough-desire which determined the course of my life and work through the first sixty-five years will bear watching. After all, they are playing on their own home field.

Hay Mow, Uses Of

Sunday, Feb. 11. When it is a rainy day, or, as today, so windy and cold nothing else is possible, Barkis and I spend her off-chain time in the barn, in the hay mow. There she is as light of foot and as eager for unexpectedly deep holes near corners and as indefatigable at galloping about and burrowing and nuzzling down as I used to be when I was comparably her age. There is no place as perfect for such purposes as an old-fashioned hay mow. This hay is the last I put in myself, loose. Hay was cut on the place for a year or two after that, but the strangers who bought it baled it and took it away. Bales provided a wonderful system for storing a lot of hay in a relatively small space without ever constituting a mow, or at least the kind of mow a child or a puppy can romp in or a pensioner get warm in. So there it is, out in the barn, this wonderful anachronism, rediscovered only because a puppy needs exercise on cold or rainy afternoons. Sitting there, with my feet deep in the two holes I have worked out for them, it is almost possible to make the mow contain the story of a life. There, with the dust-motes dancing in the stray shafts of sun, I began life as a little boy assigned to the chore of running to and fro stamping down the forkfuls the grown men hurled my way. There, between chores, I learned about different kinds of sex without knowing they were different. There I came, with growth, to take the front job in the mow and fork away the onslaught of some mature and practiced pitcher who was doing the unloading from the wagon down below. Eventually I stood down on the wagon myself, tearing the forkfuls out from under myself and tossing them up to my own children. This particular mow I filled each summer and emptied each winter for seventeen years, until I gave up the family cow and thus broke the benign cycle from field to field, condemning myself to that greatest of privations for anyone living on land, the absence of a manure pile. Now, of all this ancient grandeur, this well-ordered cycle of existence, the hay mow survives merely as an anachronistic oddity. But it is hard to imagine an anachronism with higher practical use. Where would Barkis and I ever go, what would we ever do, on a strong-winded, close-to-zero afternoon?

The One Non-God

Monday, Feb. 12. Unlike several of the elements I could worship, this has no natural use, pursues no predictable route, possesses no purpose except to rush to get wherever it isn't, and only rarely, in its relation to the human being, achieves the kind of touch that could be called benign. Even in those instances in which man, by the invention of a sail for boat or windmill, has done his best to convert it into a useful force, its performance remains rhapsodic and unreliable. Now, having lived a lifetime, I remember only one situation in which I thought it was truly wonderful and was willing to surrender myself to its spell, and that was when I was spending some glorious hours on the deck of a small freighter being buffeted by a mid-Atlantic hurricane. The rest of the time, in my life and to my senses, at least, it has been merely an idiotic intensifier of cold, a blaster of heat, a swirler of dust, a crippler of trees, a shaker of skyscrapers. If I could have my way there is no doubt I would pass a world ordinance forbidding anything higher than a gentle eight-mile-an-hour zephyr. If this writing seems in an unfriendly vein, chalk it down to the nature of the wind which was blowing outside all day long, a stiff, frigid thirty-mile-an-hour blast straight from Canada which, according to the weathermen themselves, was, with its "wind-chill factor," reducing the real temperature outside from the fifteen degrees on the thermometer to fifteen degrees below for the flesh and blood. Let it also be put on the record that this same wind blew straight through this old house, pushing all our heat from the north end, which it left at about fifty-five degrees all day long, down into the southern rooms, which were unhealthily hot, while the thermostat, halfway between these two internal extremes, kept the burner running steadily all day long. Today's wind, in addition to costing me outdoor pleasure and indoor comfort, added something like seven dollars to the fuel bill. In other days, when I was trying to save the giant ash on the west lawn, these insatiable winds cost me something like a thousand dollars before it was all over and they finally took the tree anyway. The wind is not an element; it is an insanity.

Distractions

Tuesday, Feb. 13. I have drifted into a distraction — making too much of the arrival of the mail — which leads into other distractions. This desk puts my back to the window but if I swivel halfway to the right I command the road down which the mailman comes, his lights flashing whenever he makes a stop. By frequent swiveling I can monitor his approach and be ready to pounce out the front door a split second after he begins to pull away from No. 669. Every swivel turns me away from the typewriter; my attention to what I am trying to accomplish becomes fitful; there is, for the hour or so of this special watch, very slight chance my mind will drift off into one of those reflections which occasionally produce an idea worthy of being allowed to reproduce itself on the typewriter. To the contrary, the fact that I keep swiveling to look for the mailman is only the beginning of distraction. This happens to be the hour of the day when the mockingbird is pretending to be the policeman of the thicket along the brook, when the gray squirrel forages under the feeder and looks longingly up toward the platform he can leap to when he really wants to. A chickadee brings its sunflower seed to the lilac branch that brushes against the window. The squirrel notwithstanding, a neatness of field sparrows settles down on the feeder platform. Juncos cross the lawn in flight that looks as well as sounds like a twitter. All these distractions work themselves into my morning because, in the first place, I yield to the weak waste of time involved in waiting breathlessly for the mailman as if something pleasant and interesting and unexpected and miraculous is going to find its way into this codicil life. All of which reminds me that, in the office I left, the new management's remodeling has eliminated all windows, which means that if I were still working there I would be safe from the distraction of looking out through, or for, anything.

In Envy of Real Bricks

Wednesday, Feb. 14. When I quit working in the idea factory I at first had the idea that nobody could replace me. That subsided, rather swiftly, in favor of the still comforting conclusion that nobody could fill the place as well as I had. That in turn is now yielding to a new and much less comforting realization. I am beginning to think it would never have made any difference if my particular factory had not been operating at all. Neither what I produced there, in the course of a lifetime, nor what any successors may produce there has really mattered or will matter to anybody. There are, inevitably, for the workmen involved, occasional moments of self-satisfaction — an illusion of something really meaningful being done with some degree of excellence. But the truth is that none of the idea bricks I thought I formed, none of the idea nuts I thought I fitted and turned, has ever had any real importance or made any real difference to anybody or to anything. I have stopped wondering how the factory gets along without me. I have stopped the game of measuring how well others may be doing the kind of job I used to do. I have begun to lose interest in the kind of product I used to turn out. It kept me busy. Even though my kind of bricks happened to be think-bricks, it kept me from doing any real thinking. It gave me the economics of a livelihood. But today I am close to being able to go through the morning newspaper without giving much more than a flick of mind or interest to those who are merchandizing, today, the products which were my own specialty for more than forty years. As I have begun to realize at some other moments, real bricks could at least be standing, and holding something up, somewhere.

Connecticut

Thursday, Feb. 15. Connecticut, in lexicon, consists of four of the most concise syllables ever compacted into a single word. Pronounce the syllables and they sound like what life in Connecticut, the colony and state, is supposed once to have been — prim and disciplined, with its only extrovert character showing forth in the combination of inventiveness and industriousness with which it carried out the sanctified task of insuring itself its daily bread plus a profit. Yet the soul of

Connecticut, when Connecticut was truly in its prime, was not merely a matter of stern and conservative utilitarian exterior; Connecticut life was a system which, by its disciplines, made itself work its work into returns which were privately rich and full; the balance between effort and reward was not skimped; there was a circle which enclosed both tangibles and intangibles. It was a civilization which, having comfortably selected and hoarded and protected its own values, did not care if the rest of the world failed to appreciate the rounded completeness of the satisfaction the Nutmeggers were mining for themselves. This was Connecticut as it was, and as it persisted until just a few decades ago. Since then the exterior has opened up, responding to the softening and fissuring influence of cultures which have finally mustered the numbers and confidence to step forward and put their own different kind of mark on, and values into, Connecticut life. To judge from contemporary externals, Connecticut itself is no longer sure of its ties to its own heritage and has no glimpse of any kind of new soul it may possess for the future. Its values seem to have been adulterated and its once smug satisfactions turned to demoralized doubts. Why, then, do we still manage to feel stirred by the concept and conscience of a state of political organization, geographical boundary and composite living called Connecticut? What still makes it different to us from some other similar political, geographical and social unit? The answer has to be that Connecticut still does manage, in the philosophical essentials, to change people more than people succeed in changing Connecticut. The qualitative truth is that as each new cycle of new Connecticut people has moved up front and center, it produces a new crop of political leaders and life-style setters for whom only one ethnic and cultural classification proves appropriate. They keep turning out to be Yankees running a Yankee state. Even as we wonder how they may be about to change the character of Connecticut life we find that they have fallen in love with this special compact, this fundamental order, this mixture of fumes and blossoms, this somehow indigenous dish of life which is never quite Rhode Island or Massachusetts or Vermont or any other state, and have elected to retain and eternally recreate the felt differences as if these were, indeed, proven superiorities.

The Tree and the Vine

Friday, Feb. 16. With coiled cords as thick as snakes — this is all out the window I see through when I swivel to the left in this office chair — a bittersweet vine has, for many years, been slowly throttling down a twenty-foot elm tree. Last year the elm, reacting at last to the Dutch Elm disease, which has been rioting around this place, put out its last birth of leaves and then died in midsummer with its leaves hanging brown on the tree. And the bittersweet, acting as if it, the coiled assailant, and not any invisible blight, had been responsible for some kind of victory over the elm, flowered and berried itself into a solidly massed crown, first of pale, smooth greenish-yellow and eventually of wrinkled, corrugated orange-red which has, in the right lighting, dominated the fall and winter scene on this side of the house. Now, for a few years to come, the vine which has just developed its full vigor is going to be tightening its coiled grip on the elm while the elm, no longer able to renew itself, must gradually, inevitably decay, perhaps to the point where the vine is, for a final, poetic justice change, holding up the tree. I feel inside, like the old tree, never destined to be very tall and now forbidden to grow any more, while all the late-flowering parasitic ambitions of my pensioner imagination are making a sudden effort to overcome, hide, and yet still pinion themselves to the interior disintegration which is surely taking place. One day the elm will come down, porous and crumbled. Meanwhile, it feels good still to be gripped, firmly, by something, even late-flowering dreams.

A Turn of a Screw

Saturday, Feb. 17. If this sounds gleeful, so be it. I have scored a small but significant triumph in the very area — that of service — where we pensioners are most vulnerable. About thirty hours ago the oil burner cut itself loose from the house thermostat and began running the temperature up to ridiculous heights. This meant that the second thermostat, which was in charge of operating the burner for hot water purposes, had taken over and gone berserk. Its malfunction was caused by the fact that the water in the special tank where the hot water coil is located had drained out, leaving that tank at a temperature low enough to keep activating the hot water thermostat. The cure, as performed yesterday, was to let more water into the whole furnace system until the hot water retort tank had been filled again, and then to draw the furnace water back to normal operating level. This we did yesterday. This afternoon, however, the burner was overheating the house again. The service man repeated the process of yesterday. As he worked, I kept asking him if there was not some simple way of cutting out the operation of the hot water thermostat if, as seemed likely, we were confronted with the tank emptying itself again for some mysterious reason. He gave me no answer. Several times he gave me no answer. Then, watching him, I noticed that he took a turn of a screwdriver in a certain slot when he wanted to test whether the upstairs temperature thermostat was operating properly. I pounced on the maneuver and found that, if the hot water situation recurs, it need cause no night or holiday emergency call. There is a screw I can turn myself. Counter clockwise, I think. *Moral:*

Even the occult mysteries of the service world will yield to close, persistent observation of the high priests of plumbing at their rites. We pensioners do not have to be as helpless as we seem. Beneath the mumbo-jumbo there are sometimes simple answers and cures even a novice can find.

The Splurge

Sunday, Feb. 18. During our routine pensioner week we have learned to do with simple, often leftover meals which hold our grocery bill down to an average of twenty-five or thirty dollars a week. If we could calculate this for every week in the year we would be making sense in relation to our fixed rate of income. But periodically we splurge. Sometimes, as on a weekend when someone is coming home and we enjoy having with them a special roast or steak, it is totally justified. Children do many things to repay us, many times over, with many kindnesses throughout many years — by still enjoying our home, by still regarding it as their own, by caring to come. To splurge for such a homecoming makes so much sentimental sense it also has to be ruled economic sense. But then there are those much less logical times when, without any excuse except that we ourselves are suddenly bored to the point of rebellion, suddenly sick to the core of our spirits with the prudent business of managing a tight ship, we blow dullard weeks of thrift on some insane moment of luxury. With steak or lobster or thick lamb chops we pretend, for a moment, that we are somebody else. The moment we have made the expenditure we realize that we have not changed our identity or station in life; we are still, too late to do anything more than make a valiant effort to enjoy our mistake, retirees on a fixed income in an inflationary economy. But here some partial confessions are in order. We do somehow manage full enjoyment of the rich food. We do somehow, even after we look the dire financial consequences squarely in the integer, manage to convince ourselves that our wild moment of luxury was something we needed and deserved. Pensioners do not survive by penury alone, and sometimes a spree, a wilful moment of simulated luxury, can qualify as a basic necessity.

The Safety Element in Failure

Monday, Feb. 19. "He always cracked on the brink of success." When, the other day, a staff psychiatrist from one of our state institutions was interviewed about the factors leading up to a tragic end for a bright young inmate, he was also talking about people not in such institutions. The young man in question, he said, was frightened of the outside world, and the peculiar nature of his fright was that he had a dread of "making it." Reading this made me realize that this "cracking on the brink of success" is something of which others are capable. Sometimes it has been at the brink of victory in a game of tennis; more importantly, it takes over, this reluctance to win, at that point in a pursuit of my own ambitions when one final clear-headed effort might see me through to one of my goals. At such points I have a talent for turning irresolute and behaving as if I were an instinctive enemy to my own interests. Now this particular news item helps me understand why. Failure is always a safe, familiar, no-risk refuge, a known experience; it focuses no new or testing responsibilities upon one. Success, on the other hand, is unknown territory and a high-risk business; the very life-style it imposes is full of relentless demands for even better performances and achievements. If I should now find myself actually getting close to the brass ring in some of the post-career ambitions I have been confiding to myself in this diary, would I not then have some sub-surface instinct to fudge it all up and retreat, as perhaps I have done all my life, to the comparative security of never quite making it?

The Sign of the Redwing

Tuesday, Feb. 20. Of all the signs and markers that have kept life going for us over the years, picking us up out of our doldrums and setting us off on new leases of hope and expectation, the blackbird with the red epaulets has become our favorite. This morning C put her head out the door and heard the first 1973 redwing. She called to me and I stepped out into the driveway. From somewhere across the road just to the east the first sound of oncoming spring repeated itself over and over. I was, to tell the truth, a little bit sorry it had happened so soon. Not that the bird was particularly early; one year the redwing put in an appearance on February 11. Today is closer to the date that would prove average over the years. But it is early for my state of mind. It seems only yesterday that, back on last Labor Day, this new chapter in my life opened and it seemed a matter of great moment and perhaps great doubt whether I would wear and struggle and strengthen my way through these new conditions until I encountered, yet one more time, one more spring. Now this perhaps over-anticipated period of test and challenge is receding behind me before I have even managed to experience it very deeply. Now, before I am really ready, it is being signaled that apparently I am going to make it through this new kind of fall and winter into the beginning of another earth cycle. Bearing such tidings, this is the most welcome of all the redwings of all our springs. It and C and I, fates willing, are going to make it again, we and all creatures and all things, and the earth itself. Back in September, I hardly dared think about it, I was so unsure.

My Country

Wednesday, Feb. 21. We were a fortunate, innocent generation, we who grew up with "America" as the unofficial national anthem before either the inner cancer or the outer barbarism of the nation-form of existence had begun to exact their critical levies upon this particular nation's capacity to believe in itself. Then indeed, in a mood both sublime and effortless, this was a bucolic, sweet land of liberty embellished by rocks and rills, and just to take breath in it and sing a sane succession of notes at the opening of a school day was an experience in privileged, sacred emotion. It is no full description or analysis of what has happened to us in our nationhood to say it may have coincided with the switch from "America" to "The Star-Spangled

Banner," but the change was at least symbolic. It was accomplished by a pressure-group perversion of the processes of democracy; it moved the nation's throats into a jangled and difficult and always strained celebration of martial violence; the very manner in which it prevented any audience from ever finishing in any unison either of pace or range made it more an exercise in discord than an expression of unity. Whether the song did it or not, that is where we are. The association we have with ourselves, with a certain government and inside a certain geography, is now an anachronism. Today we recover the soul we used to have for America only when we fall in love with, as another bucolic ideal to be protected and preserved, that beautiful blue globe the astronauts saw whenever they looked back on their journeys to the moon, and when we begin to conceive of all the people living on that blue globe as a blessed band of brothers whose destinies are linked more closely than the destinies of those who stood together at Bunker Hill or signed together at Philadelphia. This country — my country at any rate, and yours too, if you really come to terms with your own inner-vision certainty of what has to be — henceforth grows great and strong and beautiful and capable of winning and taking our love and loyalty in proportion as it moves to metamorphose itself from the nation-larva, with its creeping self-sufficiency based on defoliation, into the winged beauty that lives only by and for the flowering of its universe. This new vision of ourselves is where the song is, whence the lift and lilt will come if they are to come again, where the greatness may develop, where we may once again feel love for a concept which engulfs us.

Stray Comment From
the Dog Barkis

Thursday, Feb. 22.

Why I make a fuss over people:
They get lonely chained to their lives all day.
If I don't make a fuss over them, who will?

The flat top model:
They made this doghouse themselves.
They didn't know how to make a real roof.
This has a flat top.
When I lie on top of it I can see more than when I lie on the ground.

A man's life:
I have a friend who lives down the road. He never gets off his chain. He never gets to run in the fields. He never gets to chase a fluffy cat. What a man's life he leads!

Running fast:
No matter how fast he runs, I can always catch him.
No matter how fast he runs, he can never catch me.

How to train people:
Always hold the leash tight, and don't hesitate to give it a hard, sharp pull.

When you give a command, bark loud, as if you mean it.

When a person does something right, reward the person with a friendly paw and a lot of kisses.

Don't expect people to be able to concentrate on any one thing for too long a time. One short lesson a day is better than repeated drills.

For best results, all serious training efforts might as well be postponed until the person has grown up beyond the irresponsible, impulsive type of behavior. It does not really pay to try to train anybody under thirty.

This Life I Love

Friday, Feb. 23. This will have nothing to do with that final terror, assuming there is consciousness at that moment, but it has to be reported that I have begun to have thoughts in which I apply to myself, without too much panic, the inevitability of an end. Perhaps, even, there is a touch of resigned relief, as, thinking of this or that obligation, or even thinking of such ambitions and desires as are surviving into this pensioner stage, I suddenly remember that, in the words mortals reserve for self-comfort against the component aggravations of life, "this too," this time meaning life itself, "shall pass." If, in such thoughts, one is a little less frightened than one expects to be, it can only mean he is growing a little bit weary. I have not changed any belief or philosophy. It is simply that, whatever may lie in that moment, or beyond it, I am beginning to have the beginning of a feeling that I have had almost enough on this side of the experience. I do not know why this beginning of a feeling should now arrive; I am working almost as much as ever, and the way I feel, so far at least, is that I am more happy and interested and perhaps concerned with vital things than ever before. Still, at this moment when life seems to be full of at least a new kind and style of richness, there comes that occasional flicker of a thought. It will all be over, and that may not be such a bad idea. It is just a thought, and if I really face into it, as I have now done by putting this much about it down on paper, I begin to choke up and feel passionately sorry for myself that I must ever leave a life I love so much.

The Age Gap Narrows

Saturday, Feb. 24. At lunch Friday, J admitted that he had observed another birthday this week. When he said it had been his fiftieth, it surprised me that he was that old. There is, you see, more than one fallacy in the way we oldsters age-rate other human beings. If they are our contemporaries, we look at them as if they had grown old while we ourselves have somehow escaped that fate. We also have a distorted impression as to the ages of those coming after us. For a long time, on one side of a psychological line, they continue to seem unbelievably (comparatively) young. But eventually, as with J today, our image of them may suddenly alter. They catch up with us oldsters. The age gap between us does seem to grow smaller and smaller the more our ages progress. When I was forty and J was twenty-five the gap was tremendous; I was the mature man, he was the youth. The disparity, the old man - young man relationship, still held when I was fifty and he was thirty-five. But now that he is fifty and I am sixty-five the age span between us has suddenly dwindled and we are both, although I might not say this directly to him, old together. Later that afternoon, I finished a birthday letter to A, out on the West Coast. This is her thirty-ninth birthday. She has always, of course, been our little girl, and that is still the way I miss her, as if, instead of having gone to California and fallen in love with the man just right for her and produced a family of handsome sons, she were merely unaccountably late in getting home from school on a day when I needed her to help plant my corn. But now, writing to her, I could feel the beginning of a new relationship. We are getting close — rather she is getting close — to the time when we will no longer be so much parents and child as adults together. She is catching up to us, as J has begun catching up to me. If we all manage to live long enough, we will all be the same age and nobody will feel older than anybody.

Things Not Likely to Happen Again

Sunday, Feb. 25. The arrival of a book one cannot put down.

The discovery of a real new friend.

Swinging conquest in the field of sex.

The experience of eating, playing or using muscle without an uneasy awareness of the possible consequences.

The rapturous sensation of a well-deserved success in professional career.

The joyous, cloudless anticipation of the arrival of guests.

Any undiluted innocence, hope, confidence, trust, belief, certainty of opinion, finality of judgment, or any unqualified acceptance of any religion or philosopher.

Any improvement in tennis game.

Any improvement, for that matter, in anything I do, be it physical or mental, social or solitary, work or play.

Any kindness and help from someone older than I am.

How come, then, that with so much subtracted and never likely to be encountered again, there still seems to be so very much left?

Among Things Left,
a Snowdrop

Monday, Feb. 26. I notice, looking over yesterday's list, that I was careful not to include, among those things that would never be happening again, any such entries as "first redwing blackbird" or "first peeper" or "first robin." The first redwing blackbird was heard, and chronicled here, six days ago. As for the first robin, he is usually the same impostor, the all-winter all-weather fellow I saw flying low over the pond ten days ago. But even while I was compiling yesterday's list there was, right on this desk, looking at me out of a small vase, the first snowdrop of 1973. It was brought in by C and put on my desk as a token of spring to come and a remembrance of things past. And, quite obviously, the fact that this sort of thing does happen to me, and could continue to happen to me, provided one answer to that question I was asking here yesterday — how come, with so much being subtracted from life, there still seems to be so very much left? A snowdrop, the first snowdrop of a new spring, can be a very big deal. It has just happened again, and it can happen again and again and again.

Fiscally, a Beautiful Month

Tuesday, Feb. 27. Every way you calculate, February is a banner month for the pensioner. The pension itself, from the office, and from Social Security, is exactly the same amount as for every other month. But, except for a few obligations which are also calculated on a flat monthly basis, like a mortgage payment or a telephone bill, the February pension checks have a little less expense to carry. They have to set the table nine fewer times than do the long months' checks. There are fewer days for heating the house, fewer gallons of gas to buy, fewer hours of electric light and television operation. So February takes it a little easier on the pension check than any other month. At the same time February is kind to the pensioner in the matter of Social

Security regulation of his supplemental income, if any. If he is still on a payroll of some kind he has to worry that the presence of five payroll days in a month may take him over the dollar limit of his permissible additional income. But February is incapable of having five Fridays in it. Or, if the pensioner is self-employed, he has to guard against the possibility he may exceed the magic number of forty-five hours of work in a month. This danger is lower in February. The month which happens to be the shortest month of the year has other potential charms. It can bring back the redwing. Or it can feature, as it did this afternoon, the first effort of the song sparrow to recapture its trills. It has Groundhog Day and Valentine's Day and Lincoln's Birthday, and it used, before secondhand automobile sales were invented, to have George Washington's Birthday. It is also, for the particular situation of the pensioner, the most fiscally beautiful of months.

Should One Ever Visit
the Old Office?

Wednesday, Feb. 28. The circumstances that led to my "retirement" when I had always thought I wanted to die with my full job on were not sufficiently pleasant to make it even thinkable, for a time, that I would ever go back to the office as a friendly, sentimental visitor. Lately, however, I have begun to have stray thoughts about what it might be like to drop in and see how the old co-employees are, what the new ones look like, and how things are going in general under the new management. This is a good place to lay down the law to myself. I am not to do it. The reason I am not to do it is that I can still remember just what it meant in the past, and how I reacted, when some former or retired employee appeared back on the office scene. Our mood was not one of welcome but of resignation. We felt required to ask, but not to be interested in, what he was doing. We always felt, somewhere in the atmosphere, his potential criticism of something we might be doing differently than he had done it. We had, the moment he appeared, put on defensive armor against such criticism, a rough-edged armor which had, as its last resort, the cool inference that this was, after all, no longer his business, but ours. I don't believe there ever was an instance of a retired employee just dropping in to see how things were going that didn't set off a time clock ticking inside everybody, measuring, sometimes with patience, but sometimes with increasingly obvious gestures toward some piece of work waiting to be done, just how long this interruption was going to last. To think that, if I should now become the visiting former, the welcome would be any more genuine, the routine questions of me any more sincere, and the silent wave of relief swelling through the office the moment I left any smaller, would be the most nonsensical of self-deceptions. I myself, on the job, wouldn't have given two cents to see me, the ex-associate, standing in front of my desk. I must be very sure I never go and stand there, that idiotic grin on my face, waiting for somebody in the new generation to ask why I don't sit down "for a few minutes."

1040 Once Again

Thursday, March 1. Making out an income tax return remains, to the last, a sordid, cheapening experience. For most Americans it is a toss-up which they regret the more — the compulsive, timid little lies woven into their returns, or their neglect of all the sharp angles they, in their innocence, or their incompetence, never know how to exploit. The IRS has seemed to understand, from my homemade, unprofessional returns, that it was dealing with a hapless and only routinely deceptive amateur, and has, sportingly, recalculated my forms only when it could discover I had overpaid for some silly, sloppy accounting reason. But today, despite this good relationship in the past, I was all fear as I took up what may be the last full-blown, consequential return I ever have to file. There ought to be a refund calculable, out of this past split year during which I went off the payroll. But it would be foolhardy to get in trouble now when I may be about to slip out of the clutches of the IRS forever. With such thoughts in mind I began this afternoon, and nearly completed tonight, my work on Form 1040. I feel like a sap and a criminal. I am cheating, but not enough. I have always had some moralistic resentment for the cleverness of those characters who were smart enough to find loopholes and stratagems to cut their taxes legally. But I myself, for a piddling influence on the final amount of tax I pay, can't resist claiming to be a little more charitable than I am. What I really ought to do with this last return, from which a fat refund would be so pleasant, is to invoke all the strategies and calculations I have avoided over the years. In order to do that, however, I would have to get professional help. Receipt of such a totally different kind of return from me might startle the IRS into wondering just what has been going on all these years, and my efforts to make a big legal grab now might wind up in my being caught in all the little white imprecisions of my past returns. I am going in on my usual performance, missing all the smart big savings, making, I am sure, a few childish moves I would never like to have to explain under oath. Why, at this late date, should I change my whole life plan?

A Tumult of Redwings

Friday, March 2. By mid-morning yesterday the temperature was on a quick impetuous climb. By mid-afternoon it had reached sixty degrees and it was possible, for the first time this year, to sit outdoors, motionless, and still feel warm and comfortable. While we sat on the low brick wall down by the pond, the redwing which had made itself audible, but not visible, on February 20 and on several subsequent mornings, appeared and took a high poplar perch and let us see the spreading of the wings play its part in the release of the song. In a few more minutes there were redwings all around us, and the once lonely voice had been multiplied into a roundelay that kept wheeling its way around the pond until one didn't know for sure whether it was the song or the world that was turning. But whatever the source of the increasingly delirious spin, there was no doubt that blood and pulse and lung and hope and desire and courage were all beginning to wing into the pace and feeling of one more big round of life itself. Today it is cool, and gray outside, and the season is moving more normally, but moving.

Club Dinner

Saturday, March 3. The one stand-out luxury of our lives before and after retirement has been membership in Neipsic, the tennis club. We maintained it last year when we knew retirement was coming, and we will keep it this year, even though the $125 for dues will not come easy. So far we have no intention of resigning in order to get back our original membership investment of three hundred dollars. Last night, attending the annual club dinner, we discovered, or reaffirmed, two non-tennis advantages in membership. Going to a club dinner for a price the committee has negotiated is an economical way ($5.80 last night) to dine out. And participating in the annual business meeting of a tennis club offers a rich demonstration of the way all life operates. Tonight the effort of the club leadership was to find out whether the members really wanted to install night lighting. By the time proposals for another new court and a swimming pool had been thrown into the race and a proper discussion of what kind of question should be put to a vote had taken place, and then two show-of-hands votes had been taken and tallied (each followed by remonstrances from people who confessed they really hadn't voted the way they wanted to), there had resulted that typically amiable state of confusion in which the uncertainty of the answer had begun to cloud and obscure the original question. We all went home without the slightest idea of what we had voted to do about lights, or a new court, or a swimming pool, and that kind of uncertainty is, we are sure, not only the summit experience of club membership but also the closest insight we are ever likely to achieve into the mysteries of group action. Later somebody from high office will tell us not how we voted but what is going to happen.

Stanley Williams Was Right

Sunday, March 4. From English courses at Yale, I remember three things: John Berdan's scornful prescription for modern writing (1926) which was "one hand on the penis and the other on the pen"; Alex Witherspoon's marvelous weaving of real life and circumstance into his conducted tour of the seventeenth century; and Stanley Williams's patient, wise remark to an impetuously romantic honors student to the effect that said student would, by the time he had reached his forties, be making the relatively prosaic

Wordsworth, instead of the tropically lush Keats, his personal idea of a great poet. For more than two decades now that erstwhile student has been proclaiming that, so far as he is concerned, Wordsworth is the greatest, and "Tintern Abbey" the greatest poem ever written. Somewhere in this diary there has to be a day and place for celebration of the inexhaustible richness of those "Lines Composed A Few Miles Above Tintern Abbey, On Revisiting The Banks Of The Wye During A Tour — July 13, 1798." Ever since I first really read the poem, which was indeed sometime in my forties, "pastoral farms, Green to the very door" have been the ideal main view in every imaginary landscape. On the human landscape, "little, nameless, unremembered acts Of kindness and of love" have occupied a similar position. In dream and aspiration, "that blessed mood, In which the burthen of the mystery, In which the heavy and the weary weight Of all this unintelligible world, Is lightened." In time of sorrow, "The still, sad music of humanity" offering the solace of understanding and companionship. In time of peace and euphoria, that ''sense sublime Of something far more deeply interfused, Whose dwelling is the light of setting suns, And the round ocean and the living air, And the blue sky, and in the mind of man; A motion and a spirit, that impels All thinking things, all objects of all thought, And rolls through all things. Therefore am I still A lover of the meadows and the woods.'' I find, right now, that I cannot go on in this business of random quoting; the poem becomes too dear and meaningful to be summarized; I will go back to the beginning and read it all again. Please, dear reader, do the same (the only thing this diary will ever ask of you) so that you may absorb instruction how to ''let the moon Shine on thee in thy solitary walk; And let the misty mountain-winds be free to blow against thee.''

The Red Tape Murders

Monday, March 5. Today I came into contact with what I am sure is the single greatest killer loose among American males — the trigger to heart attacks, the spawner of ulcers, the incitement to cancer — and, for the greater torture of those who survive such dangers, the great reservoir of all arthritis. This single greatest threat to the health of the American male lurks inside the forms, regulations, interpretations, confusions, near-contradictions and invitations to false assumptions which comprise the federal government's relation to the finances of its subjects. The other day I waded, blind and fearful as always, into my income tax return, remembering, as I did, how the mere experience of having an internal revenue man come into his office

377

and go over his books triggered a heart attack for a friend of ours. Today, having received a form from the Social Security people requesting a report of my income for the past year, and finding myself totally lost as to how to handle the fact that I had retired and gone on Social Security for only part of the calendar year, I visited the Social Security office for help. The people there were kind and courteous as they told me things about the Social Security system it had not occurred to me to ask about, and about which it had not occurred to Social Security to inform me when I was filing my retirement action. I still can't explain it in detail, but what was happening during the first twenty minutes of my interviews was that, owing to the complications in the regulations and to my own inability to understand how they applied to my own situation, I seemed about to lose, in total, the some $1,080 C and I received in Social Security payments for last October, November and December. This, while it lasted, was a threat to my experimental financial position so devastating and cruel it had me trembling. And I have been trembling ever since over the potential precariousness of the way out of this dilemma — the way out which gradually opened up as the nice people in the federal office struggled with the twin problem of my situation and my lack of understanding of it. But the point I make is this: whatever else happens in this connection, today's experience was one of those life-shortening experiences that take another little degree of sureness and pace out of the functioning of the heart and make every part of the system more vulnerable to whatever may be lurking there. Now, as I am about to go to bed, I have an intense arthritic pain in the back of my throat. If I am lucky and have a good night's sleep it will have disappeared in the morning. But I still do not, and will not, understand all the intermeshed regulations by which I am supposed to live in the future, or which, for a while today, were about to slaughter my new way of life. And being under the domination of forces one cannot understand is trauma, psychosomatic trauma.

Call Us Pensioners

Tuesday, March 6. Readers of these entries may have noticed that their author has not yet once chosen to identify himself or any contemporary as a "senior citizen." Nor has there been any toleration, by even the most incidental kind of use, of the term "Golden Ager." If it came to a choice of terms on that level, the preference would be for the simple "old folks" that was so serviceable to all the generations before the modern insistence on life-by-euphemism took charge. Much of the writing that is done about us old folks turns, if it somehow does shrink from "senior citizen" and "Golden Ager," to the word "retiree." The big national organization that wants us all to be members calls us "retired persons." My favorite, and the one that has steadily worked its way into these entries, is, by its strict definition, the opposite to a euphemism. I like using the word "pensioner." Yet the dictionary classifies a pensioner as a hireling, a hanger-on dependent on some patron's or relative's charity, or as a medieval mercenary who was sometimes called, perhaps in a euphemism of that day, a "gentleman-at-arms." Perhaps the appeal of the term to someone often given to the practice of false modesty is that it does strike a tone of humility, so that, using it, I can smirk inside at the thought of what a gay deception my boundless inner ego is playing on the world. But I prefer to think that I am somehow really satisfied with the unpretentious democracy of a term which, in these days of Social Security for almost everybody, can be used to describe both the technical status and the style of life for so many people.

The One Elixir

Wednesday, March 7. Has there ever been a man of sixty-five not willing to try to find the fountain? That is a confessional question leading into an admission that, yes, there did come that phase, preceded by much family jocularity when this diarist submitted himself, mixing surface protest with secret hopes, to the potential powers of Geritol. I was foolishly willing to have a miracle occur even if came by sheer quackery. The fact that, in my case, no miracle did occur is not to be taken as a reflection on the particular product. I already had my hang-up on and my belief and trust in Vitamin C; there is a question how many psychosomatic masters one individual can carry on an arthritic back. Still, from this personal experience, the verdict has to be that Lawrence Welk does more for old age than his product does. The reasonable, logical aim has to be restated: It is not to recreate youth, but to lend beauty and satisfaction to the various phases of an inevitable recessional; not to deny old age, but to exploit its own particular opportunities. The only reliable elixir ever concocted for life after sixty-five wears the corny old patent label of love; now, more than ever before, the gentle affections, no longer merely sentimental adornment, constitute the very structure of life.

The *Times* as a Newspaper

Thursday, March 8. A whir and a blur emerging into episodic clarities of type and information and then quickly disintegrating back into the pulp and confusion from which it was manufactured — that is the newspaper.

We who have been in it consider it the most thankless and the most rewarding of professions. We wear exorbitant prides in an effort to hide and ignore the humilities enforced upon us. We try, when we are at our best, to maintain some balance between the freedoms we claim society owes us for its own good and protection and the responsibility we ourselves owe society for the good of our own blackened souls. We in the trade expect the best performance from the likes of us to come in the New York *Times's* product, and that is why the routine of this ex-newspaperman's retirement day begins with the two-mile round trip necessary to get the New York *Times.* Yet it is probably in the modern character, or shifting character, of the *Times* that our profession now encounters its greatest sense of insecurity. The once safe anchorage is no longer surrounded by the breakwaters of stuffy tradition. The institution's once imperturbable façade has been lowered to let the reading public see its passions showing. The newspaper that used to report and judge events in reflection of the character in them now brings its own character to the reporting and judging of events. Where there was once a distinct and reassuring probability that, if the *Times* saw and reported, that was the way it was, there has come to be a possibility that the *Times* itself has developed a certain way of seeing and reporting. As against the deadpan truth over which there could be no factual controversy, there is now offered a higher brand of truth that depends upon some element of philosophy for its validity. In the view of the philosophy present in the *Times* itself and among its personnel, this brand of truth is what is good for the public to have, and providing it is a new and higher and more dedicated kind of journalism. But occasionally, in a startling, heart-rendingly temporary moment of reversion, one of the *Times's* pundits slips out of his recognizable routines and takes a discussion stance in which he at least pretends that his own philosophy and that which antidotes it both have equal right and footing at the threshold to the reader's mind, and we

385

have, in this temporary flashback, a measurement of something lost.

Birds

Friday, March 9. We can swim in the sea and we can burrow into the earth but we have never been able to beat wings into the sky. The creatures that can fly on their own wings are the most variable, graceful, and beautiful of living things. To befriend them and support them is a way of gaining for ourselves a distinguished group of dependents whom we display proudly for our friends, over whom we fancy ourselves possessing and playing a life-and-death role, and to whom we dispense food, not so much to keep them from starving, as we may pretend, but to bring them closer to ourselves for our own selfish scrutiny and eye-possession. They, for their part, repay our imperfection of motive with generous and iridescent splendors; there is no loveliness on all earth like the indigo the bunting flashes into the sun, the blush around the throat of a waxwing, the trim, chaste neatness of a field sparrow with its perfectly proportioned smallness, its suggestion of having always just emerged from some apricot-tinted bath. To suggest that the birds, by such generosities, over-compensate for the poor services people render them is not to discount entirely the dedication of the true watchers and feeders. They also — who can identify a mere flash in the thicket or one note whispered across a meadow — are a rare breed, whose expertise we lazier and less competent people can merely envy inside our own exasperating lack of precise certainty about anything beyond robins. We were always hoping, during those years when bird watching seemed a special privilege that had to be borrowed or stolen from the rest of the day, to come to the time when we could at least be master of our own thicket. Now we have had time enough to know that that time will never come. The remarkable thing is that a relationship so imperfect and incomplete on my part can fill so large a part of my life. The more credit to the birds who, in my book, more than any other species, give life to the world.

Out of the Blue

Saturday, March 10. A few of these pieces have included observations and perceptions which, however they may have appeared or appealed to the reader, were at least a delight and a surprise to the writer. They have been those realizations, those turns of a phrase, those dips into some hidden but cosmic knowledge which come "out of the blue" and "in from left field" and "in over the shoulder" and somehow flow through the fingers into the typewriter keys in the same electronic instant in which the consciousness becomes tinglingly aware of their approach. They perform, these unpredicted flashes of discovery and relevance, varied services. They disclose to me things I did not think I knew about myself. They glorify, by their blinding instant verities, the remarkable abilities of the feeling and sensing and analyzing apparatus we carry around inside our individual compartments in the great universal mind. By explaining at least parts of things to us, they give us a taste of the peace of understanding and a touch of the triumph of having closed our own mental and sensory grip on some wonder of life. Every time one sits reflectively at the typewriter there is this chance one may encounter some cosmic entelechy striking a surprise *aperçu* into the mind-sense chemistry of the moment. The highest excitement that ever visits life comes not on any field of physical contest but in the motionless, reflective pause. The typewriter, or the pen, diary-bound, make handy, functional accessory-impetuses for such a moment, but an unashamed, uninhibited daydreaming can approach it too. You set the mind on reflect; out of the nothingness which may be, instead, the universal consciousness, the miracle heads your way.

To Stop the Killing

Sunday, March 11. The first and only murder trial I ever covered used the testimony of one of the participants in a grocery store holdup to send the other one to the gallows at Wethersfield. One had what brain there was for the pair: he planned the holdup; he bought the gun; he put the gun in the hand of his accomplice; he pushed his accomplice in through the door; and then he provided, in return for a light prison sentence for himself, the testimony that hanged his friend and accomplice. This was all a perfectly legal disposition of a case, but complete misjustice. If there had been no compulsion to try to hang somebody for the murder, however, the apportionment of guilt and punishment might have been more even-handed. Some twenty years later I had to live and write my way through the story of the Rosenbergs who, if they were guilty, were guilty only of supplying secrets in peacetime and guilty only of supplying such secrets to another nation with which we were not at war but which was, in legal fact, our ally, both circumstances under which no executions for espionage had previously ever taken place. Now, twenty-five years after that, I have grown totally sick of the combination of vindictiveness and superior righteousness that considers itself entitled to take the life of a fellow human being under any conditions, and I am, therefore, a prime example of what some defenders of capital punishment call a loss of national courage because it shrinks from giving society the tough brand of loyalty it must have if it is to survive. It so happens that I, or the chromosomes in me, measure the health of our society exactly the other way. It has, for some years, been a matter of breath-holding hope to see a public trend away from capital punishment. But now what might have been the moment of greatest triumph has turned itself around toward new disheartenment. The Supreme Court has ruled against the death penalty, but has ruled by side-door technicality rather than by full and honest challenge to the right of the state to take life principle. And what has ensued, when there might have been psalming and rejoicing, is the appearance of a sudden, fierce drive among the state legislatures to draft detours around the Supreme Court's technicality so that the death penalty can be legalized again. Unbelievably, states that were, before the Supreme Court decision, on the verge of abolishing their own death penalty provisions, and states that had been going along for years quite content not to execute the tenants of their death row cells, are now acting as if they cannot wait to be taking lives again. I want no part of it. I do not want to pay my mill-fraction share of the cost of the current or the rope. I do not want to have to admit that the civilization with which I have traveled this life can retrogress so easily. This is the hardest thing of all to take in these farewelling years when one would like to have a few good things certain — the discovery that society is once again trying to compensate for the fact that some of us are murderers by making murderers of us all. There are times when a continued belief in the improvability of man depends upon a fierce act of will. I keep making it. Sooner or later sanity and humanity will resume their self-imposed obligation to try to stop the killing.

March Rain

Monday, March 12. Eventually there comes a rain such as that which invited the Canterbury pilgrimage. Instead of reminding one of the comforts of getting inside and dry it invites one to walk on endlessly, taking it in the face, watching it bead itself on the briars and the small branches, or pock into the open water which has begun to edge around the dwindling ice floe still holding out in the middle of the pasture pond. This year this rain came today, which is early. But it was not ahead of the rest of the season. At the farther end of today's walk in the rain there were small honeysuckle leaves flecked out in the warm sidehill pockets of the woods. It was several days ago that C reported daffodils on the move. Now that I am indoors and warm and dry after this first free and happy walk in a 1973 rain, I know there is no longer much doubt about it. The season moves; the calendar and the weather weave together; the way I realize this, in sweet March rain, is not by any mental process but by a feeling of pull-up which begins down in the viscera, travels up through the lungs and heart, makes the throat want to shout, tilts the head back and open to the spray, and persuades the veteran he is re-enlisting for at least one more campaign.

The Science of Leisure

Tuesday, March 13. Some of the first people we hear from in the retirement state are the experts who work hard trying to tell us how to employ our newfound leisure. We are grateful for their efforts and, occasionally, their insights. But we fault them, too. The first thing they do is make leisure itself seem to be some mysterious, almost burdensome science when, in reality, it is composed of very simple things. Leisure is bare skin being caressed by warm sun. It is cushions on a couch. It is food and drink at the elbow. It is being unhurried in the bathroom. It is a margin of time between one involvement and another. But to picture retirement as a state in which one automatically has unlimited time for that kind of living is both a philosophical and a pragmatic error. Leisure, the freedom, is like all freedoms in that it cannot exist except in relation to fixed occupations, duties, and obligations. When and if these can be limited, the dividend can be turned into leisure. But such leisure ceases to exist unless it keeps bumping itself against and reinforcing itself through contact and conflict with things that must be done. To begin to plan for leisure time, then, one aims first to make sure of a continuing context of chore or obligation. It is in helping us organize the prerequisites to leisure that our experts perform their best service. They suggest to us new occupations we can substitute for the old obligations that used to keep us busy. They help us invent new chores to be the bread for the leisure sandwich. If they, and we, are successful, we wind up still very much occupied with things to do and not much more time or opportunity for sun, cushions, and Roman orgies. The deep dark scientific secret for leisure time is not to have too much of it, and the happiest retiree is the one who discovers that he is busier than he ever was, so busy he still can't begin to find time for all the things he was going to do. To find leisure, look for work.

Half Time

Wednesday, March 14. Today, March 14, we made, once more, our annual short-breathed walk up and over the hill for the pussy willows which, as of this writing, have already replaced last fall's bayberry in the pewter pitcher under the dining room mirror. On the way back down the hill we heard the first peeper of the new spring. Later, sitting by the pond, I noticed the narrowing circle of center ice revolving, at noticeable speed, in a lag-unison with the water under it — the most primitive and yet compelling demonstration that we live on an earth that moves by spinning. This confluence of signs, the seasonal and the eternal, is so powerful it puts a momentary clamp on all other sensations. Now, as it relaxes, it is time to note that I have, season-wise at least, come past the halfway mark in this experiment in pensioner living. Six months have gone; this is the 192nd day. By this time I should have some idea of how it is going; the next six months may, if I don't watch out, pass just as quickly. But the only way I can sum things up is to say that there have been almost no definitive answers. The thoughts committed to this paper have been suggestions more than they have been determinations. The hard economic problems — the question of our long-range solvency, the problem of how to keep up the house and furniture, the decision whether I must eventually try for a greater income — all have been evaded and postponed, as indeed I intended they could be when I gave myself this experimental year. For the end of this inconclusive half time score there is, however, one footnote — "bottom line" is getting to be the phrase of the moment for the statistic that counts most — which has a strong claim to the right to say it tells the whole main crucial part of the story. I don't believe I have ever been happier. I don't believe C and I have ever found more pleasure in each other's presence. If this kind of life doesn't work — and the next six months may demonstrate that it can't — it should. I know now, at least, that it is worth fighting for, worth putting everything into. I know it is an opportunity, not a fate; not a deprivation or a diminishment, but an enrichment; a beginning no less engaging because it must be the beginning of an end. The most frequent thought I have had in this first half year is that I should have begun doing this a long time ago.

The publishers hope that this Large Print Book has brought you pleasurable reading. Each title is designed to make the text as easy to see as possible. G. K. Hall Large Print Books are available only from your library or through the Large Print Book Club. If you wish a complete list of the Large Print Books we have published or information about our Book Club, please write directly to:

G. K. Hall & Co.
70 Lincoln Street
Boston, Mass. 02111